More COFFEE with Nonna

Stories of my Italian Grandmother

Vincent Iezzi

SERVANT
BOOKS

PUBLISHED BY ST. ANTHONY MESSENGER PRESS
CINCINNATI, OHIO

Cover illustration by Jim Effler
Cover and book design by Mark Sullivan

Library of Congress Cataloging-in-Publication Data

Iezzi, Vincent M.
  More coffee with Nonna : stories of my Italian grandmother / Vincent Iezzi.
     p. cm.
  ISBN 0-86716-712-2 (pbk. : alk. paper) 1. Christian life—Catholic authors. I.
Title.

BX2350.3.I492 2005
248.4'82—dc22

                                                              2005016198

ISBN 0-86716-712-2
Published by Servant Books, an imprint of St. Anthony Messenger Press.
28 W. Liberty St.
Cincinnati, OH 45202
www.AmericanCatholic.org

Printed in the United States of America
Printed on acid-free paper

05 06 07 08 09 5 4 3 2 1

CONTENTS

God smiles two times a day.
Every morning He smiles knowing that we will
love Him during the day and every night He smiles
because He is so pleased with the love we gave Him.

—*Domenica Maria D'Amore ("Nonna")*

DEDICATION

For my brother Anthony and sister Diana
and for Mom, Aunt Jenny, Aunt Rita and
Uncle Lawrence who had more coffee with
Nonna than any of us.

ACKNOWLEDGMENTS

The author would like to thank his lifelong friend,
Chay Sabatini, of New Jersey, for his help.
He also thanks his wife for her patience and love.
Most of all, he gives great, special thanks to his God,
who gave him his Nonna.

INTRODUCTION

When Nonna came to this country, her goal was simple—she wanted to live better. Life on a farm and shepherding did not hold much of a future for her. But even though Italy could not hold her, she never left it behind, for she brought it with her to America. In everything she did, she was Italian.

America held some sad times for her. By the age of twenty-five, she had borne the loss of her first daughter and she had been widowed two times, being left alone to raise her children. Her brother, sister-in-law and other relatives helped as well as they could, but it pretty much came down to Nonna and Nonna alone.

In America, she found a strange prejudice toward her and her people. She suffered being called an "alien" by a country she believed was hers. I recall her once saying to me, "I am so American that I sometimes feel everyone else in this country is a foreigner."

Over the years, she worked hard as a tailor in several clothing factories and she earned money by baking, crocheting and knitting. But she worked hardest at being a mother and later at being a Nonna (Grandmother). Her life was one of complete sacrifice for her children and grandchildren. It was nothing for her to give up things that she needed for the needs of her family.

Nonna was not a tall or big woman. She was short and small, grown close to the earth. She was a woman of many facets, but above all she was a woman of God. She didn't need theological explanations or logical theories—God was simply God in all His Mysterious Trinitarian Persons, and He was deserving of her love, respect, adoration, and devotion. Her relationship with God was so very plain and childlike that undoubtedly this is the reason her stories have been so easily understood and loved.

She was a woman of customs and traditions. She followed the dictates of her traditions to live life close to God and His Church. Holidays and feast days were celebrated with the sense of being a part of God's life and of life in the Church. She followed the examples of her ancestors in sharing, caring, and loving others, always finding a bit of truth in everyone and in everything.

Many who have read *Coffee with Nonna* have found her to be a typical Italian grandmother, but to our family she was unique. No one cooked as she did, or sewed, crocheted or knitted as she did. No one understood other people as she did, and no one had the patience that she had. No one worked as hard or regretted as little as she did. No one was as grateful for the small things that came her way as she was. None of us saw and understood life as she did.

She became a warrior only when someone else was in harm's way or when unkindness was being shown. When she was the warrior, it was best to get away from her as quickly as possible.

Nonna was very patient, but she absolutely could not tolerate unkindness. This seemed to be something that was deeply carved into her soul. To her, "kindness" had many tentacles that stretched out into the world of virtues to capture many other virtues that she freely associated with kindness. Having a deep sense of hospitality or being grateful and appreciative was part of kindness. She pushed the limit of kindness to include thoughtfulness, consideration, concern, gentleness, respectfulness, politeness, and many, many other qualities.

The one or two times I remember being really punished by Nonna was when I was unkind or when I had ignored one of the other virtues under the big umbrella of kindness. As a result, kindness was the one virtue that I always thought of first when dealing with other people. As I grew up, I gathered all of kindness' companions and made them a part of my living journey.

Because of her limited education, Nonna was hungry to learn. She loved to listen to her grandchildren speak of what they were doing or learning in school. At times, she would just sit and watch us work our way through math problems or watch us struggle with history or geography questions. If we ever asked her for help she would say, "Well, let's work this out together." She would let us figure out the answer and then say, "Of course, that is the answer. See how smart you are." Many times, she would ask us to read out of one of our textbooks as she readied the evening meal and occasionally she would stop her cooking and comment in wonder at what she had just heard.

"That makes sense," she would say, or, "That is so true."

Her respect for education extended to our schoolbooks and to any book she saw. Once, I caught her sandwiching a book between her hands. She held it with reverence, almost imploring it to speak to her or pass through her hands into her mind. Never, ever would she tolerate the mishandling or ill treatment of a book. This was a sacrilege in her eyes.

Conceivably, that is why she was such a good storyteller, an Aesop, because she had so much respect and admiration for the written and spoken word.

Of course, Nonna was not just a good storyteller; she was the very moral thread that made up our family. There were many times she would say things, just sayings, that later in our lives we found to be so wise and true.

Many years after her passing, the emptiness is still there; it is always there. And even after years and years have passed, and she is recalled often as being "a good woman," "a kind woman," I know that she is in heaven blushing from embarrassment.

One thing I know for certain, when I am called by God to come to Him, I will see Nonna. And no matter how old I may be, I am sure she will come over to me and hit me on the side of my head and say:

Voi e la vostra bocca larga. ("You and your big mouth.") And she will smile and blush.

I hope that will be my only punishment, for if God is merciful to me, and if I deserve it, He will return me to my youth and to the back kitchen of our house on Dickinson Street and allow me to share more coffee with Nonna.

CHAPTER ONE

• TZIZZIE—ONE OUT OF THE POT •

Her real name was Rosa, but we all called her Tzizzie. She was Nonna's sister-in-law, the wife of my great-uncle Tony, Nonna's only brother.

"Tzizzie" was an endearing name reserved only for her by all of Nonna's children and grandchildren. In like fashion, all of Tzizzie's family called Nonna "Tzizzie."

In Italian, Zio means "uncle" and Zia means "aunt." Now you must understand that I had hundreds of "uncles" and "aunts," many of whom were not really uncles and aunts at all, but first cousins or distant cousins, some many times removed, of my grandparents or great-grandparents. Out of respect—with no deviations ever, ever permitted—they were to be called Zio or Zia.

My friends often made fun of me because I seemed to have so many aunts and uncles, while they only had a dozen or so. To make matters worse, almost all of these relatives lived within a ten-city-block radius of our house, which meant they visited often, very often, and I saw them many, many times walking the streets. Even my brother Tony and my sister Diana grew up thinking all of these people were actual uncles and aunts, and I had to clear up the confusion years later.

Though all these relatives were respected greatly…there was only one Tzizzie.

Tzizzie was special to me. She always made me laugh because she loved to laugh. It seemed that when she and I were together we were constantly laughing about something we did or said or had heard said.

Often, the rest of the family would just look at us and shake their heads in disbelief. They gave up trying to under-stand what we were laughing about and just let us have our good times. And because laughter is so contagious, they soon would be laughing with us, which caused Tzizzie and me to laugh even harder.

She had a way of spoiling me, and because of this I loved to go to her house, which I did as often as possible. When I visited, inevitably I would be asked to stay, and if she came to our house she would "kidnap" me and take me home with her. Nonna gladly let me stay or go. It gave her a chance to have one less child to care for.

When Tzizzie's children, my cousins once removed, came home at the end of the day, they would continue spoiling me. When Uncle Tony came home from work all was complete, for I could never do wrong in his eyes and I always got anything I wanted.

Whenever I had dinner with Tzizzie's family, one of her sons or daughters, my older cousins, would walk me home and always we would stop for ice cream, "water ice," or cakes before we would continue the six-block walk to my house.

Burned deep in my memory is the picture of Tzizzie coming down her stairway carrying a bucket with a mop standing upright inside it. In her other hand was always a broom, and tucked tightly under her other arm was always a dust cloth. The broom reminded me of a lance from one of the knights of King Arthur's court for she had used it as a weapon many times. I had seen her use this broom to chase stray cats out of her backyard and the big black dog back up the street. Once I saw her use it on one of the fruit vendors (we called them "hucksters"), because he had sold her spoiled fruit.

When she did housework, Tzizzie's hair was always wrapped up with a cloth that somehow had the same pattern as the apron that covered her housedress. I never learned the secret of how she matched those two things so flawlessly.

So I have many warm and hilarious memories of Tzizzie. Out of all the memories, the event known as "One Out of the Pot" remains my favorite.

It was just before the outbreak of World War II. By

Church law, Catholics were not permitted to eat meat on Fridays. Fish or shellfish were most frequently on the menu for Friday dinners.

On this particular Friday, Tzizzie had bought two dozen live crabs for dinner. As she had carried the two brown paper bags into the house through the living room, one of them broke. All the live crabs fell to the floor and crawled and scampered in twelve different directions throughout the house.

Tzizzie screamed but quickly recaptured her senses. She ran to the kitchen, threw the other bag of crabs in the icebox, and ran back into the living room, shouting for me to help catch the crabs.

"Be careful!" she yelled in Italian. "Don't get pinched. It is very painful and sometimes you cannot shake them loose."

We ran in all different directions, looking under this chair and that table. We found some crabs hiding defensively in the corner with their claws open, and some in the dining room, and even some climbing up Tzizzie's home-knit lace window curtains. It seemed like we spent hours searching and finding and carefully capturing the crabs.

Finally, we counted our catch—and found we were one short. We continued our search, but we were going over and over the same places without success. We ran out of places a crab could hide, so Tzizzie decided that the fish man had made a mistake and had given her eleven, not twelve crabs.

"I will deal with Angelo, the fish man, later, when I seen him next week," she said with a tight lip. "Come Vincenzo, it is late and we have to kill all the crabs and cook them for tonight's dinner."

So we began the task of shelling the crabs, an art I had learned from Nonna and others in my family. When this task was completed, Tzizzie washed the crabs very carefully, seasoned them, and threw them in a pot to boil. She then began making the gravy (tomato sauce). When the gravy had stewed long enough and had the right taste, she married the crabs and the gravy together and cooked them even longer as she began boiling water for the store-bought spaghetti.

All this time, I sat watching Tzizzie work around the kitchen from my favorite place: on "the bench" on top of the water radiator. "The bench" was a long, thick, wooden board that sat on top of a long water radiator in the kitchen. I thought it was so neat to sit on this board, and I always sat at the end of the board that was farthest from the gas range and kitchen sink and nearest to the back door of the house. From this spot, I had the best view of the house. I could look out through the dining room into the living room and I could easily see who was coming into the house and what was going on in the rest of the house while keeping an eye on the activities in the kitchen.

The rest of the afternoon passed, and Tzizzie continued to mutter that Angelo had cheated her. I could tell by the tone of her voice and the frown on her face that Angelo was in big trouble. I felt sorry for him.

Soon, my cousins began coming home from school and then from work. Each homecoming was exciting for me for these cousins were my favorites. They always made me feel like a grown-up.

Tzizzie and Uncle Tony's oldest daughter, Rachel, was my godmother. Out of respect, I called her Commare Raykel because I couldn't say her name properly in Italian. The title "*commare*" was used to set special people off from the rest of the world and Commare Rae, as I later called her, was always a special person to me.

Finally, Uncle Tony came home and the family was completely assembled. Soon after his arrival, it was time to eat.

On the supper table, besides the dishes, utensils, and glasses, we found the bread and the wine. The bread was always a large, hearty, round loaf and hard-crusted, that sat solemnly on a plate covered with a big white linen napkin.

The four corners of the cloth were lifted and folded over the top of the bread to cover it. These folds revealed four small slithers of the bread's crust and they formed the Sign of the Cross. I had been told that when this folding was done, the bread became a sacred item. We were brought up respecting bread. It was never to be mistreated or in any way desecrated. When bread was placed on a table, it was never to be turned upside-down; the bottom of the bread was to rest on the table. If ever you dropped a piece of bread, you were to pick it up immediately, wipe it off and kiss it before consuming it. Bread was never to be thrown away. If it got hard, you created bread-crumbs from it, a duty that was reserved for the children in the household. Crumbs from the table were given to the birds. If, God forbid, the bread "went bad" it was kissed, placed in a brown paper bag, wrapped carefully and—though I never saw this being done—quietly placed in the trash.

The wine at our table was always a hearty, homemade, dark red wine and it had to be placed in the most expensive or delicate glass decanter in the house. The decanter did not have to be crystal, just good cut glass that cost a few pennies more than other containers. When the decanter was filled, it was placed by the bread—it looked like it was guarding the gentle, nourishing loaf. The wine was never chilled but kept at room temperature, ready for consumption.

Family members were called by first names to supper. The table was set and only the two items—bread and wine—sat in the center of the table. Needless to say, these were symbols of the Eucharist, and, though no one ever pointed this out, we all understood. Everyone in the house would sit in his or her assigned seat. When everyone was seated, Uncle would simply say "*Grazie, Dio, per quello che ci avete dato*" ("Thank you, God, for what you have given us.")

Everyone would respond, "*buon appetito*" or "*mangia bene.*" Tzizzie then would put the meal on the table.

I, of course, sat on the radiator and to my right sat Uncle.

Tzizzie sat across from me, next to him, with her back to the rest of the house.

Uncle took the large round loaf of bread, cut the first piece from it and then turned the loaf over to Tzizzie. She cut the bread for the rest of her family, holding the round loaf on its side. With her left hand she held one side of the bread while the other side was pressed against her chest. With the bread held in this position, with great artistry, she began sawing the knife toward herself, cutting long strips of bread. For the longest time I could not bear to watch her or Nonna do this because I was so afraid that they would slash their chests. But as my faith in their skill grew, I watched with total amazement. (I was told one day by my godmother, Commare Rae, that only Italian woman cut bread in this manner. The only reason they never get hurt is because when bread is being cut, special angels rush from heaven to watch over the mothers to protect them from being cut. It must be true because it looked really dangerous and unwise, and no one ever got hurt.)

After the bread was cut, the large bowl of macaroni in crab gravy was placed on the table. We ate in silence. It was an unwritten law that we remained silent until Uncle Tony spoke and picked the topic of conversation. As soon as he said the first word, everyone talked and laughed and the wonderful joy of an Italian family meal burst wide open. I listened to my relatives talk about their days and their grown-up problems and I was happy that I was still young and not in school or working and I was free of all the troubles they had.

Tzizzie rose from her chair and announced she was going to get the cooked crabs. Like all Italian wives, she did this small act every evening as part of her wifely and maternal duties.

My cousins continued to jabber, tease and talk as Tzizzie left the table and went to the gas range to get the large bowl of cooked crabs. My eyes followed her because I loved to see the proud and joyous look on her face when she returned with the meal she had prepared for her family.

With Tzizzie away from her seat, I had a clear view of the dining room, and from the corner of my eye I saw something moving.

There, creeping defiantly on the tips of its legs and with open claws, was the last crab from Tzizzie's broken bag. He walked slowly but brazenly toward the kitchen.

Tzizzie returned carrying the bowl of crabs, and from the corner of her eye she, too, saw the crab. She quickly looked at me. She raised her eyebrows and opened her eyes wide to show her surprise. Then she drew her lips tightly together, puckering them up as an order for me not to react. I wanted to laugh at her facial antics, but I knew her expression said that I was to remain serious and calm.

She placed the bowl of crabs on the table, sat down and placed her finger to her lips, confirming that I was to remain quiet.

The family continued with their talking. I lowered my head, not wanting to be caught smiling, until I heard Tzizzie cough and begin to gag on a small piece of bread she had tried to eat in an effort to act normally.

Everyone at the table reacted with concern, but Tzizzie waved them off. She grabbed a napkin and, with tears in her eyes, she looked at me. Her face was red and shining and I knew that behind the curtain of the napkin was a big smile and a muffled laugh.

Within in seconds, without a word or a signal we both broke into deep uncontrollable laughter.

The rest of the family looked at us, surprised, and then began to smile. They had no idea what we were laughing about, and of course we were beyond any rational ability to explain ourselves to them. Soon everyone was laughing with us.

Finally with tears in her eyes and with a red face, Tzizzie announced, in Italian: "*Penso che, per grazia di Dio, uno dei granchi sia scappato dalla pentola*" ("I think, by the grace of

God, one of the crabs got out of the pot.") With that announcement she and I collapsed into hysterics just as my Commare Rachel and her sister, Mary, spotted the crab making its way onto the kitchen floor. They began shrieking loudly. Everyone jumped up, and total chaos broke out. They chased the crab, but he scurried away in panic and disappeared once again into another part of the house.

Tzizzie and I, alone at the table, laughed until we had pains in our sides and more tears in our eyes.

CHAPTER TWO

• JUST ADD WATER •

The aroma of morning coffee brewing makes the ringing alarm clock more pleasant, but even that can't compare to the smell of things being cooked or baked early in the morning.

The smell of bread baking gave me the feeling of warmth, home and stability. The smell of baking cookies or cake gave notice of a special day such as a birthday or an approaching holiday. Every Sunday morning, the bubbling of tomato gravy and the savory smell of meatballs being fried filled the air with the tender comfort of family and food.

Many in the house, when waking up to these aromas, jumped into action to start the day. I, however, preferred to stay in bed, secure in the knowledge that something good would be part of my day.

Every Sunday, even before the war, the family—including all my aunts and uncles who married into the family—came to Nonna's for the one o'clock Sunday dinner. This tradition was never broken or altered. Only serious sickness or death or being away at war was an excuse. To this day, no matter who the cook may be, waking up to the smell of something cooking brings back memories of Nonna.

One cold March weekday, the smell of baked cookies and cakes plus the smell of gravy from the stove woke me up.

"*Buon giorno.* Hurry get up. *Oggi è la festa di San Guiseppe,*" I heard Nonna say from the back kitchen of our house. Immediately, the house came to life. I heard my cousins jumping out of their beds and rushing to the bathroom to wash and dress quickly.

"Nonna, Vince isn't getting up," one of my cousins shouted.

"Vinzee!" I heard Nonna say, and I was pretty sure she was smiling for she knew how I liked to linger in bed enjoying all the smells of cooking. But I knew how important that particular day was to Nonna—and to all Italians.

As Nonna had announced, it was a good morning and a good day because it was the feast day of Saint Joseph. We had the day off from school, but before we could think of our own enjoyment, we had to go to morning Mass at King of Peace Church where the Franciscan sisters and our classmates were waiting for us. Then we hurried home for a breakfast of bread, butter and coffee before a full day of celebrating.

It was a day filled to the brim with Italian customs and traditions (Americanized somewhat for convenience).

Nonna told us that the celebration of the Feast of Saint Joseph had begun in Italy in the Middle Ages. At that time the people of central and southern Italy were suffering from a great drought and they asked Saint Joseph for rain. They told him that if he was able to make it rain, they would hold a large feast every year thereafter in his honor. Well, the rains came and from then on, March 19, the feast day of Saint Joseph, became a day when Italians feasted.

In Italy, there are big parades after Mass and *La Tavola di San Giuseppe* is set outside of the houses so that all passers-by and relatives can eat and visit. In America, "the table of Saint Joseph" was set inside people's houses.

Food of every kind was cooked and baked. Orange slices were cut thin, slightly roasted and sprinkled with sugar. Stalks of sweet fennel and oil-cured black olives were served first, followed by homemade beef or chicken soup with *pastina, acini di pepe* or *orzo*. If I was lucky, sometimes my favorite—hot *pastina* with melted butter—was available.

Soup and dishes of pasta, platters of fish, vegetables and omelets were all put on the table of Saint Joseph. You could have any one of these or all of them, just as long as you ate something.

Later, sweets and special cakes were offered—*zeppole* (cream-filled pastries, often called "Saint Joseph's Cakes") as well as *cavione* (small, deep-fried pieces of dough stuffed with various fruit preserves).

Of course, there was Italian wine, some sweet homemade liqueurs, and always coffee.

The jets on the gas range burned all day cooking, heating and reheating food for the table.

The only ones exempt from this feast day were families who were "wearing black." If you had suffered a death in the family and were still mourning, you could not be expected to celebrate, not even for Saint Joseph. It was an unwritten rule of respect to remain sad for a whole year.

There was another unusual twist to the day: no cheese was ever eaten. Nonna told me this was a custom because Joseph could not afford cheese for Jesus and Mary. So parmesan or ricotta cheese was not to be used on any macaroni. Instead, grated breadcrumbs were sprinkled on the macaroni, because the bread symbolized what Joseph could afford to provide for the Holy Family.

If a family needed or wanted a prayer or favor from Saint Joseph, they would build an altar on a small table near the "food table," in Joseph's honor. Because it was wartime, every mother had an altar. Many of these altars were very elaborate, but Nonna, as always, made a very simple one.

"Plain, just like Saint Joseph was," she told us, though this did not stop her from using her best Italian linen cloth to cover the altar table on which our statue of Joseph stood. Nor did it stop her from using her best candleholders, long candles, red vigil lights and the freshest flowers she could buy. If fresh flowers could not be found, she would resort to a bouquet of artificial flowers instead.

What Nonna did pride herself on was the food table, which she graced with even better linen, our best china and silverware and, of course, the best food in South Philadelphia.

For days, Nonna and my mother and aunts would clean and reclean the house. And for days Nonna baked cakes and cookies. On the night before the feast day, she would start cooking the rest of her food.

On the day itself, we, her grandchildren—washed and perfectly dressed—were told to watch our manners and always be friendly, helpful, respectful and gracious—or else. We were to be with Nonna all day helping to greet and serve our guests.

"*Fai subito!*" We heard Nonna say, and we hurried down the steps into the warmth and delicious smells of the back kitchen.

"*Buon giorno, Nonna,*" we all said as we raced to the clothes closet, got our coats and bundled up for the cold March weather outside.

Nonna, in her hat and coat, stood waiting patiently in the living room. Soon we assembled around her, and we embarked on the long, cold walk to church and Mass.

No matter how fast Nonna and I would walk, my cousins always seemed to be able to walk faster. "They have longer legs," she would tell me, but I never believed this because they were just as short as we were.

When we finally arrived at King of Peace, Nonna sat in the back of the church with her Sacred Heart Society lady friends. We went to sit with our classmates under the watchful eye of the nuns, who for that day had traded their stern looks for gentle smiles.

After Mass, Nonna's friends didn't stand around talking outside the church as they usually did because this was the feast day of Saint Joseph, an all-important day to the ladies. They all had to hurry home and prepare for the "table."

Though no one would admit it, there was a rivalry among these ladies. Often they would make quick checks ("visits") to each other's homes to see what the opposition had.

Going home, Nonna and I kept up with my cousins.

When we arrived, we rushed through our breakfast and immediately began doing the last-minute things. Some of my cousins were ordered to make the beds in the bedrooms and close all the doors. Others were told to "clean the bathroom and leave the door open." I was given the all-important job of making certain the living room was OK.

Within a half hour, our house was thrown open to everyone who wanted to eat. Those who entered the house would give the greeting, *Viva San Guiseppe!* (Saint Joseph lives), which triggered the reply, *Vive per sempre!* (He lives forever).

It was not unusual to hear this greeting shouted intermittently throughout the day: whenever anyone was so moved, they shouted it out and the others replied.

Most of our guests were neighbors and relatives, but it made no difference if you were friend or foe, rich or poor, white or black, Catholic or non-Catholic, just as long as you ate and celebrated our Joseph. Many came and did just this. So many came that sometimes our visitors stood to eat because we had run out of chairs on which to sit.

One of the highlights of the day was the arrival of our pastor, Father Cosago, who was expected to visit every home that had invited him. At each house he was expected to eat something and, of course, he was expected to bless the food table.

The other highlight would be the arrival of several Italian nuns from our parish convent. These sisters would make the rounds, hoping to enjoy a small taste of the "old country." Sometimes a few of the Irish nuns would come along to try "just a bit of what you have."

One year, Tzizzie asked Nonna if she could help her because her parish was not Italian. So the Italians in Tzizzie's parish did not have anything as elaborate as our parish did. All her Italian neighbors went to the houses of relatives or friends to celebrate "the feast."

Nonna was pleased and gladly welcomed Tzizzie, but her joy quickly faded when Tzizzie said she would make the soup at home and bring it over after she had gone to Mass at her parish. Making soup was one of Nonna's favorite things because it was an ancient dish, a poor man's dish. She knew it had washed the stomach of many great and poor people. But she could not hurt her sister-in-law's feelings. Reluctantly, she agreed.

I was delighted that Tzizzie was coming. It added to my special day to have two women I loved so much with me.

So after Mass at her parish, Tzizzie arrived at our house in a car driven by one of her 4-F nephews. She hurried immediately into the back kitchen to the gas range with her heavy pot of homemade soup. Soundly depositing the pot on the gas range, she turned the jets on very high and began to reheat the soup, stirring it with a long wooden spoon.

Nonna was too busy to notice that Tzizzie had arrived with only one small pot, in comparison to the many larger-sized pots Nonna would have prepared. I knew immediately that Tzizzie had not made enough soup to last the day. It was such a cold March day. The first thing that would be requested by our guests, after coffee and some sweet liqueur, would be soup.

As I watched, Tzizzie cheerfully hummed a melody from one of Verdi's operas. With her left hand on her hip, she stirred the pot with her right hand. As she happily stirred, her dress and apron swayed in time with the melody she was humming.

Occasionally Tzizzie stopped and tasted the soup, then added pinches of seasonings. Not wanting to disturb her happiness, I just remained silent, kept my fears to myself and left her to the back kitchen.

Thirty minutes later, I peeked into the pot and saw that the soup was just about half gone.

Just then, Tzizzie came into the back kitchen. From the look on her face I could tell she was very worried. She grabbed my arm as I passed her with a few clean dishes in my hand.

She whispered furtively, "Vincenzo, do you think I made enough soup?"

"No, Tzizzie," I said timidly. "Nonna would usually have three or four big pots made and sitting on the side."

"Really?"

"Yes. It is cold out and a lot of people ask for soup to warm up."

"How many more people will be coming?"

"Oh a lot of our family has not yet arrived. A lot of our Commares and Compares have not arrived and Father Cosago and the nuns from the school have not come yet."

She fell into a chair, totally crushed and panic-stricken.

"Oh my God, what am I going to do? I don't have all the things I need to make more soup. I would have to go buy them and it would take me at least an hour to make more. Domenica will never forgive me."

She bit her lower lip and moved her eyes quickly. She put her hand over her mouth and then dropped it to her lap. She began to wring her hands together as her mind began to cast about for a solution to her dilemma. Suddenly her face brightened. She ran to the metal cabinet nearby and pulled out a large saucepan. Briskly, she walked to the kitchen sink, drew water and carried it back to the gas range, pouring the water right into the pot of soup.

"Domenica does this all the time with her coffee, so...." Looking down at my shocked face, she smiled and said, "Vincenzo, whatever you do, do not let Domenica know what I have just done. You understand? You promise?"

I nodded my head and ran quickly from the back kitchen, wanting to distance myself from what I had just seen.

The guests continued to arrive and we continued to serve them coffee, pasta and soup. More came and still we served them coffee, pasta and soup.

Father Cosago arrived and the house went into high gear. Everyone greeted him warmly.

"*Viva San Giuseppe!*" he shouted, and everyone laughed or smiled or gave the greeting back to him. He refused an invitation to sit down and went over to the table of Saint Joseph. The house fell into total silence. After a short silent prayer asking Saint Joseph to bless all our hard work and good hearts, he blessed the table and everyone shouted again, "*Viva San Giuseppe!*"

I could see his hands and face were red from the cold.

"Vinzee, go get Father a hot cup of soup," Nonna ordered.

I stood frozen and didn't move.

I was torn between telling her about the soup or allowing Father the unpleasantness of having Tzizzie's soup.

"Go, Vinzee. Go."

I walked to the back kitchen, slowly and deliberately filled a soup dish with some soup and, with a soup spoon in hand, walked carefully back to the dining room.

As I handed the soup to Father, I closed my eyes tight and gritted my teeth. I didn't want to see his reaction, and I didn't want to say something to him that would make Tzizzie mad at me. When he took the dish, I rushed to a corner of the living room from which I watched what was going to happen.

Father, wearing a big smile, slowly scooped up a spoonful of soup, and after blowing on it to cool it a bit he took a sip. His smile faded, and he slowly and diplomatically put the dish on a nearby table. Nonna saw this, and her smile faded faster than Father's had.

I ran into the kitchen and got a cup of warm coffee for Father and took it out to him.

He thanked me by pinching my cheek very hard. He always did that to me and it always hurt when he did it!

He took it from me gratefully, but carefully sipped it to make certain it had a taste.

About five minutes later, he left. As soon as he was gone, Nonna rushed into the back kitchen. I followed her. I found her standing at the Tzizzie's pot. She looked confused.

"Vinzee, is this still the only pot of soup Tzizzie came with?"

I nodded my head and started to back away in the direction of the dining room. I knew I had to get away.

"There are no other pots?"

I shook my head and continued to retreat.

"How can this be? With all our guests this soup should be gone. Have you had any of this soup?"

I shook my head.

She reached for the wooden spoon, scooped up some soup and tasted it. Her face exploded in shock.

"*Buon Dio!* It is water!" Nonna quickly made the Sign of the Cross. "Oh God, I need a miracle."

I said nothing.

"What could be wrong? Rosa knows how to make soup; what could have happened? Oh, and poor Father Cosago. God only knows what he thinks of my cooking, of my house and family." She said this aloud, but she was really talking to herself.

Then, realizing I was still there, she added, "You are to say nothing to your aunt about what I asked you or just found out. Do you understand, Vinzee?"

I nodded.

"Go," she ordered. With no regrets, I hurried from the kitchen.

Trying to forget all I knew, I busied myself carrying trays of cookies and cakes around to neighbors, strangers, friends and family. As I walked around being a good grandson, people greeted me and asked about school and my mother and aunts who were all working and complimented me on being a good boy. My mind was elsewhere, however, namely in the back kitchen.

Minutes passed. Finally, I had to return to the kitchen to tell Nonna that three nuns from my school had arrived. I found her standing by the stove. Her lips moved in silent prayer as she continued to stir and stir the soup in Tzizzie's small pot.

"Nonna, the sisters from King of Peace are here," I said with trepidation. But a smile came over her face. She stopped stirring the soup and with a small nudge to my back, she pushed me ahead of her through the dining room and into the living room, where she greeted the nuns warmly. She even embraced them, which I didn't believe was the proper thing to do.

(Nuns were never to be treated in such a friendly manner but rather as near-saints. They were a few inches above us. They even glided over floors and across streets like saints would. For the longest time I believed they had no feet. When they walked their long dresses made shushing sounds; clinky-clanky sounds came from their big rosaries or from the keys that hung from the clothesline ropes around their waists. They always seemed so perfect, so starched, so unbending. Everything about them was precise and correct. They always had the best handwriting and always spoke softly and politely—except when they were teaching. Then they had all the power of the universe in their voices. I had an awesome respect for them, but I had a deeper fear of them.)

Quickly I found myself a corner of the room, knowing that I was to remain distant, quiet, and respectful because I was in the presence of nuns. Standing there, half-hidden, I was mesmerized by them. I concluded they truly were out of place in my dining room, in my house.

Nonna was very happy in their company and she spoke in Italian to Sister Mary Teresina and Sister Mary Zita and they translated what was being said in English for Sister Mary Thaddeus.

"Would you like a cup of coffee?" Nonna asked.

A wise offer.

The nuns softly declined.

Then I heard Nonna say, "Sisters, you must have something warm. How about a nice hot bowl of homemade soup? It will take the chill out of you."

I looked at Nonna in total disbelief. Perhaps she didn't like the nuns as much as I thought she did. To offer them heated water from her great kitchen was an insult to them, to herself, to our family and even to me. I was certain they would remember the bad-tasting soup, and in school they would take out their revenge on me.

She excused herself and left the room. Because I was afraid of the nuns and had nothing to say to them, I scurried behind her. She quickly collected three clean bowls and spoons and placed them on a serving tray. Going over to Tzizzie's pot, she scooped up three healthy servings. Carrying them on the tray, she proudly walked into the dining room.

I could have sworn that she was humming as she left me standing in shock.

My image of Nonna's pride in hospitality and perfect cooking, and her total concern for others crashed before my eyes. Her greatness began to dim. I was on the verge of tears when I decided to climb onto the chair beside the range and look inside the pot.

It was still full. I got a small spoon nearby and tasted the soup. I almost fell from the chair—it was delicious!

Nonna had asked for a miracle and her prayers got her one. God did a miracle in my house.

I jumped from the chair and slowly positioned myself in front of the gas range. I stood looking at the pot, knowing that it was now a religious article. I could not stop looking at it or stop the thoughts that were racing through my head.

What am I supposed to do, now that I discovered a miracle? I have to tell Father Cosago and the nuns. The Church will have to know. I will probably have to go to Rome and tell everyone about it. I will have to talk to the all those bishops and cardinals. My God! Even the Pope! Nonna will become a saint and they will have holy cards made up with her picture on them and her statue will be in all the churches. Worse, she will be taken from us. I won't have her to talk to. What am I to do?

I could feel my heart pounding in my chest and heard it echoing in my ears.

Slowly, I backed away from the range and finally fell into a chair far from the miracle soup pot. Tears began to well in my eyes, tears of fear.

I didn't want Nonna to be a saint or my house turned into a shrine and I did not want to go to Rome.

Mussolini was there!

The war was there.

I would be held a prisoner!

I swallowed hard and tried to act like an adult.

But this is God's doing, and Sister said when God does something for us we should always shout with joy. But I can't shout with joy, so I should tell someone and let him or her do the shouting.

I felt faint but I knew I had to go tell the nuns right away. They would call Father and he would call the bishop and cardinal and life would never be the same for Nonna, my family or me.

Weakened, drained and shaken, I slowly rose from the chair and began to walk into the dining room and surely into a different life. That was when I saw them in the trash—the empty cans of store-bought soup!

Instantaneously, my obligation to report a miracle was dissolved. I grinned giddily, loving the wisdom and resourcefulness of my Nonna. Now I felt God had done something for me, and I really did want to shout with joy.

So I walked into the dining room, walked directly up to Nonna and kissed her firmly on her cheek.

"What's the matter? Are you sick? You look flushed."

"I'm okay. I just had some of Tzizzie's soup," I said coyly.

A big understanding smile came to Nonna's face, and she pulled me to her side and playfully hit me on my behind.

By three o'clock the feasting was over. Nonna, Tzizzie, my cousins and I fell into any empty chairs to relax. Nonna and Tzizzie began talking about all the relatives who had been at the feast and soon stories and news about the family were exchanged between them. It was catch-up time.

In the back of our minds was the knowledge that soon we would have to start anew. Our family workers, my mother and aunts and Tzizzie's family would soon come to Nonna's house, and they would need to be fed and to celebrate like the many others had.

"Before we start getting things ready for the family, I think I'll have something to eat." Tzizzie said as she rose from her chair and slowly walked into the back kitchen.

"All went well," Nonna said smiling broadly. "Thank God I have such good grandchildren. They worked hard feeding the hungry."

Tzizzie returned from the back kitchen carrying a cup of soup and a soup spoon. She sat down in a chair and moaned.

"Domenica, all was well. Thank God."

She brought a spoonful of soup to her lips.

"Oh, *San Guiseppe!* This is hot."

"Oh course, it's been cooking all day. Give it time to cool off," Nonna said. Then, as an afterthought, instigated by something I knew was a touch unholy, she added with a great big grin on her face, "and if you cannot wait for it to cool, just add water."

I laughed.

Nonna followed.

Even Tzizzie laughed.

CHAPTER THREE

• ALL THIS TIME •

My family was always making things.

The women were forever knitting or crocheting. They made scarves, sweaters, shawls, baby blankets and even infant clothing such as small suits and dresses. They crocheted lace tablecloths, bedspreads, doilies for living-room tables and living-room chairs. (It was very common to see crocheted doilies on the armrests of a living-room chair or on the backs of the sofas, couches and armchairs.) I even remember Nonna and many of her friends crocheting curtains for their living-room windows.

Many of my male cousins made small wooden tables, bookstands and stools. Eventually, every household in our immediate or not-so-immediate family was given one of these as a gift at Christmas.

My father made toys from wood and he made lamps from glass ashtrays that my mother proudly displayed on our living-room tables for years.

We made all these things for our own benefit, but they were often given as gifts as well. Because they were hand-made, the gifts had a special meaning: there was love in them.

The things I remember most were the things we made together as a family when everyone was pressed into service. Every man, woman and child was expected to help. Of course, every time we children had to do these things, we complained, but still we enjoyed the family atmosphere and the togetherness that surrounded these times.

First there were the "jarred" things.

Late every summer, Nonna and Tzizzie would buy crates or bushels of peaches to be cooked and preserved for next year's needs. Then they would begin recruiting members of the family by simply making an announcement at dinner that "the peaches are in the basement and it is time." No one ever had to ask what they meant. We all knew we had to assemble in the basement and begin peeling or "skinning" the cooked peaches. We also had to free the peaches from their cores and cut them in halves or quarters.

While Tzizzie supervised us, Nonna would cook her secret recipe of heavy, homemade syrup. After all the peaches were skinned and stoned, they were combined with her syrup and preserved in heavy glass jars. These were stored on the shelves in the cool back basement for the next winter, when it would be difficult to buy peaches.

If we had the money, Nonna would sometimes buy pears, plums and cherries, which we would prepare for jarring.

Our biggest yearly project, however, came when "it was time" for fresh tomatoes. After all, we were Italian, and every Italian's life is sustained by red "gravy" (tomato sauce).

Nonna would buy what seemed like hundreds of fresh tomatoes from our distant relative who had a farm. She would then cook them in pots that were so big that each of them occupied two jets on the old gas range in the basement. For weeks the air in our house would carry the sweet aroma of cooked tomatoes.

When a pot of cooked tomatoes had reached that "right time," Nonna would call for help. If you were "invited," you reported to the basement where you would find six or seven chairs arranged in a circle. Sitting on the floor in front of each chair was a large aluminum pot and on each chair was a round metal strainer with a large clean dishtowel.

You had to sit on the chair and place the strainer between your legs, holding it tightly with your inner thighs and knees as Nonna poured hot cooked tomatoes into the strainer. With care and courage, we had to squeeze the hot tomatoes, making the tomato juice fall into the pot beneath the strainer. The strained tomato "gravy" was then canned in large, glass jars with gold lids. They were put with the fruit on the shelves in the back basement for the next winter, to be used for our macaroni dinners.

Sometimes, we just had to peel the hot boiled tomatoes and she would preserve them whole in similar jars. These tomatoes would be added to the tomato gravy for extra flavoring and body.

The other big family project was the making of home-made wine, and this project belonged to Uncle Tony and his wife and helper, Tzizzie. In the backyard of his house, Uncle grew grapes. The grapevines were planted in the small "garden" that ran along the sides of a wooden fence in his yard.

The vines were strong and healthy-looking. He had constructed wooden slats from the right side fence to the left side fence and the vines grew freely up the side of the fence and along the slats, intertwining back and forth. This made Uncle's yard a canopy of "wine grapes" and their green leaves. As years passed, the grape vines began to grow into the neighbor's yard but they, also being Italians, enjoyed the invasion with no complaints.

I loved this yard because I got a beautiful feeling walking under the vine canopy. Uncle and Nonna often said that the yard reminded them of the grape vineyards back in Italy and I felt like I was a part of their past when I walked under the vines.

In the summer I loved the deep shade under the vines, where splashes of sunlight would break through the leaves and grapes. I used to run around under the vines, playing a game of tag with the sun, trying hard not to be touched by the spots of sunlight. Of course, each time the wind blew, the leaves would shift and new sunspots would be created. Uncle Tony called me *pazzo* (crazy), but I remember he always laughed as he watched me play my silly game.

The other reason I loved this yard was because I loved to eat the grapes right off the vine. There were times I ate so many grapes that I became ill, but getting sick never stopped me from trying to eat more. I would climb anything in the yard that would get me close to the grapes and just pick and eat until I was either caught or became sick.

Just before the end of each summer, things would get serious in Uncle's house. All the male members of the family (except me, for Uncle feared I would eat more than I would pick) would be called to Uncle Tony's house to pick the wine grapes from the vines. These were added to the crates of grapes that Uncle had purchased. Then, with the small wine press he had made in his basement, we would make home-made Italian wine.

Uncle Tony had one rule regarding his wine, and the rule applied to only the male members of the family: "If-ah you don't-ah make-ah da vino, you don't-ah drink-ah vino. *Tutti capito?* (Everyone understand?)"

Believe me, the rule was never altered: if you did not help make the wine, you would never be given any at dinner. The only exception to the rule was if you became ill and you had seen a doctor. Then Uncle would proudly present you with a glass of warm wine to cure you.

Those of us who were small had the important duty of cleaning the inside and outside of the wine barrels. Uncle made certain that those of us who had this job did it in short stints. "If not-ah you might-ah getta drunk-ah," he would warn.

I always had fears that I might get drunk doing this, though at the time I didn't know what being "drunk" felt like. Even if I had known, I would not have objected, because it was an important thing for me to drink wine with the family at dinner.

Drinking wine at dinner was a "grown-up" thing to do. To have my own glass of wine showed that I had helped make the family wine and that I was growing up. Of course, there was a special bottle of wine in Uncle's house just for us kids, and I now know that, like Nonna's coffee, it was watered down. But still, we had our wine. Growing up with wine as part of our meal made us respect this beverage as a family friend and not an enemy or a disease.

Finally, there was the making of our sweet liqueurs. Only the grown-ups were permitted to do this. We children were forbidden to even speak to anyone outside the family about what we saw and knew about this project even though we knew all of our Italian neighbors, friends and relatives did the same thing.

Flavorings normally used to flavor cookies were purchased from any Italian grocery store in the neighborhood. With a small bottle of anise extract, coffee extract, or mint extract you could make delicious liqueur by adding alcohol to it. The end product would be anisette, caffé sport, or crème de menthe.

Though these drinks were served when we entertained, that was not their primary use. They were primarily used for medicinal purposes. If you had a cold, you were given anisette and you would "sweat the cold out." Crème de menthe was offered for indigestion to "settle" your stomach. And if you needed energy, caffé sport was provided "to perk you up."

All these homemade things were created to make our simple lives better. The things we could wear were meant to keep us warm and the things we could eat kept us healthy. The things we drank were truly used for medicinal reasons because they were cheaper than visiting a doctor, which we could not afford. More important, they were invaluable because they were made and shared with love.

When the war came, a lot of the things we made became difficult to make because the materials were more difficult to acquire. Then, one at a time, the men in our family began to disappear. Fathers, uncles, cousins began to leave for far-away states and countries. As a family, we made many trips to the train stations for tearful good-byes. My mother and aunts went to factories and tailor shops to help the war effort. The world conflict disrupted not only the world but also my family's ways. It changed the world for America and it changed my family for we never returned to our family projects.

But the war did not stop Nonna.

One day, she announced that she had joined a group of women in the Sacred Heart Society that was making quilts for the poor. At their meeting place, they had a large, wooden quilt frame built by one of the carpenters in the parish. Nonna called this frame the "stretcher" because it held the material for the quilt in place with small tacks and wooden clamps.

At any given time these women were working on three quilts. Together they would purchase stuffing, which they called "quilt batting," gather their needles, thread, and other materials, and set to work.

They would attach the material to the stretcher, cover it with something that looked like gauze, and layer that with a thick layer of batting. Then they sewed, by hand, triangle-shaped pieces of cloth onto the material on the stretcher.

After helping make several of these quilts, Nonna decided that she would make a patch quilt for each of her daughters and her daughter-in-law. No one seems to remember why she decided to do this all by herself, but it seemed very important to her at the time.

Because she was not working with her lady friends, she had to gather the patch materials all by herself, so she pressed my mother, aunts, and other female relatives into gathering materials she would need to make the quilt.

This is the part I remember most. I helped her find and gather materials and then I helped her cut the many different patches into "pyramids."

We used old, discarded bed sheets, dresses, aprons, shirts—any old clothing that, believe me, was always in endless supply. Each discarded item was cut into patches and eventually they were sewn to a backing made of a solid red fabric that had been purchased from some dry goods store.

From a discarded cotton dress we would get hundreds of patches and from an old bed sheet, many, many more. When Nonna thought she had enough patches for one quilt she would go to the stretcher in her Society's meeting room and begin sewing the gathered pieces of material together. It seemed she completed one quilt about every nine or ten months.

During the war, bad news came often to visit us. Sometimes it left holes in our family—big gaping holes that have never been filled.

Tzizzie, like Nonna, had sons and sons-in-law in the military. One morning, while her sons were facing death on the warfront, Tzizzie didn't get up. Her death was as devastating to our family as one of our war casualties.

For months afterward, things were not right in our family. We did all the things we did before but we didn't do them with spirit. Then, suddenly, when all was so gray and sad, Nonna began making a quilt again. This time she began a little differently. She asked each of us to help, by invitation. One day at a time, she asked her nieces, Tzizzie's daughters, to come and help her, then my mother, and then my aunts.

One day, it finally became my turn. As I walked into the house from school, I smelled the coffee being made, and I heard Nonna in the back kitchen.

"Vinzee, come here," I heard her say from the back kitchen.

I found Nonna sitting at the kitchen table. She had already poured coffee into our cups. The milk and brown sugar were on the table. She was working on the patch quilt, stitching pieces of material together and preparing them for her growing quilt.

She was wearing her black dress and stockings, still in mourning because of Tzizzie's death. Black was the color all the women in the family were wearing. Though I understood the idea of mourning and I was used to their wearing black, it still made me very sad because when I looked at them, I knew the reason for the black, and I missed Tzizzie again, and more.

"Come, sit, your coffee is ready. Help me sew some pieces of material together for my quilt. It is your turn," she said, not looking up from her sewing as she pushed some fabric triangles across the table to me. Quickly, I recognized the material as having come from an old bed sheet that had once covered my uncle's bed.

Dutifully, I picked up a needle, threaded it, and began to stitch the material together, stopping occasionally to take a sip of my coffee.

"Would you like to make a visit to Uncle Tony's house tomorrow?" Nonna said, unexpectedly.

Without thinking, I first said, "Yes." Then, with some thought, I answered, "No."

"And why, no?"

"It just doesn't seem the same. Tzizzie's not there and the house isn't as happy as it used to be. I get a funny feeling when I go in that house."

"An empty funny feeling?"

I glanced up, surprised that once again she knew exactly how I felt and still amazed that she could do this miraculous thing. I noticed that her eyes were moist.

"Yes, that kind of funny feeling," I said softly.

"Ah." She sighed deeply and heavily and quickly lowered her head and returned to her stitching.

The silence between us and in the house was heavy and thick. This had been happening among all of us in the family. It was something I was getting used to but did not like. I purposely coughed to break the silence, and as I did this I looked at Nonna. She was studying me.

"Death does that, Vinzee."

"Does what?"

"It creates silence. It creates emptiness." She said this softly as she looked away from me into the stillness of the rest of the house.

I followed her gaze, thinking that someone had come into the house without my hearing him or her. No one was there. Glancing back at Nonna, I saw that she seemed to be looking for (or at) someone. As she spoke, slowly, she seemed to be talking to someone else. Her eyes and face looked lost in another place.

"Maybe the living grow silent because they are so afraid. After all, death has just walked by them, right through their house, and has rested on a loved one. As for the emptiness, well, that is something I think we make stay and grow...." She stopped talking and suddenly, like someone awakened from a trance, she sat erect and her voice changed and her tone became positive, "...and it is good. We should miss our loved ones and remember them always because they were and always will be a part of us. I have lost many loved ones, Vinzee, and I have learned that they really never leave me. I cannot see them, but they are there with me, around me. They stay and try to help the living, if God permits them to help. When our loved ones die they do not stop being part of our family. They are always part of our family, they just are not seen. They become our family's new guardian angel."

She began sewing again.

I reached for my last patch. I held it in my hand for a long time, looking curiously at my grandmother.

She smiled.

"Oh, Vinzee, you must be confused. You see, God didn't create all angels with wings. Some of them have to earn their wings. So when our loved ones die, they stay with us helping us do the right things. They give us good directions, and that is how they get their wings. People are angels because they come into our lives and walk with us. They pass through our lives and touch us. They create things, ideas and incidents that give us chances to do good. They never have wings when they are still among us. Later, they are angels, messengers of God, that He sent to lead us and direct us to good things."

She lowered her sewing on to the table and folded her arms across her chest, leaning forward onto the kitchen table.

I was forced to stop and look at her.

"Tzizzie was an angel without wings. She made us do good things and she made us laugh at ourselves while she helped us to be happy with the small things we had. She left us many memories, which cannot be stolen from us or forgotten unless we let them be stolen or forgotten. We have a trunk filled with happy, tender and loving moments with her that God was good enough to let her share with us. So Tzizzie stays with us still, only in a different way. The dead should always be with us. I remember reading somewhere that the soul begins its life in the memory of others, in the memory of those who are left living. I believe this."

She sat back in her chair. Her eyes moistened even more as she picked up her sewing and began to sew more quickly.

I returned to my last patch. We sewed in silence. It seemed like a long time, but it was only minutes.

"And she is with us and with you, Vinzee, because dying and sealed caskets and being covered with dirt cannot break the strength of love and respect that people have for each other. You and Tzizzie had a special thing together. She taught you how to love and how to respect and how to laugh."

I watched Nonna as she wiped her eyes.

What she was saying hurt her for I knew she missed her sister-in-law. But she was letting herself hurt this way so that I would understand life and death.

I think it was at that moment that I really knew how much Nonna loved me.

As I watched her, I remembered Sister Mary Madeleine saying that Jesus suffered and hurt because He loved us and wanted to make dying and going to heaven easier for us. Nonna was doing the same for me.

She glanced at me and with a feeble smile on her lips said, "It is good that we have had this little talk. Death of a loved one can be a burden, and a burden shared is always made lighter. We have shared, and it is good. Tomorrow, we will visit Uncle Tony and when you go in the house remember that it is your aunt's house too. The wallpaper and the furniture of every room in that house are filled with her laughter and her voice. Listen and you will hear her. Take a deep breath and you will smell her cooking, her fried meatballs, her gravy cooking and even her perfume. Remember these things and her soul will begin to live. Once you do this, you will know that she is with you and will always be with you."

I continued to sew, understanding all that Nonna was saying, wanting to make her words—I needed to have her words—stick in my mind.

I reached for another bunch of material that Nonna had passed to me.

My hand froze in mid-air.

I recognized the material instantly. It was from one of Tzizzie's aprons or bandannas.

"Nonna?…" I said wanting to ask if she knew where the material was from.

"Sew. Patch Tzizzie into our lives so that she will always be a part of us, warming us through this quilt."

With tears in my eyes, I tenderly picked up the material and carefully, gently, reverently, slowly pushed the needle through the material to let Tzizzie be with us always.

Just recently, the last quilt that Nonna made was finally retired from use, and Tzizzie and Nonna had been with us all this time.

CHAPTER FOUR

• SECOND-BEST •

When I started school at the age of six, I could not speak English very well. I spoke with a very heavy Italian accent, in a way that some people would call "broken English." This impediment was the result of conversing only in Italian with Nonna with whom my family lived during the war. She practically raised me and spoke mostly Italian and if she spoke English it was "broken English." I followed her example and would often say things or phrases that were imitations of her wording.

My first-grade nun, Sister Mary Madeline, would often smile when she heard me speak. She thought I was cute and my accent amused her a great deal.

I, in turn, was amused by her County Cork Irish accent. I thought she had something wrong with her tongue because I could not always understand her. She said a lot of things wrong—not like us.

So, between the two of us there was hardly any communication and, more tragically, little learning. At the end of first-grade school year, Sister suggested to my mother that I repeat the grade.

Many years later, when Sister and I met again, she told me she was amused by the certainty I had about the way I spoke. I truly believed I was speaking correctly. After all, this was the way Nonna spoke, and Nonna could do no wrong. Sister told me that I would often look at my classmates in total disbelief, amazed at the way they were speaking.

Often, I had left her trying to "unscramble" everything I said. She also admitted that she found me to be "a dear, respectful and smart lad," and the only male who ever said, "When I grow up, I'm going to marry you."

Of course, when I heard her tell me these things it only

confirmed my belief that I had been held back because Sister liked me.

I found Sister's remembrances of those days flattering. I was somewhat disappointed that she did not recall all of my proposal, for I remember saying: "When I-ah grow up I'm-ah gonnah marry you an' teach-ah you how to talk-ah like-ah an American."

By the time I got to second grade with Sister Mary Killian, I was speaking better, but my English grammar was atrocious. So Sister asked Annie, one of my neighbors who was in a higher grade in my school, to tutor me. After this, every school night, Nonna would walk me up the street to my tutor's house. I would go directly to the back of Annie's house where she was doing her homework while Nonna would visit with Annie's nice mother and father in the living room until the session was over.

Annie forevermore became a very special person to me. She was a pretty, highly intelligent, personable, sweet, kind, caring girl. Soon, of course, I developed a crush on her.

A bit later, when she was in the eighth grade, she became a "celebrity." In fact, she was the first "celebrity" I knew. She reached this high status when she was elected by her eighth-grade classmates to be May Queen. Being May Queen was a great honor. It singled out a girl to do an important thing for God. May Queens had the honor of crowning the Blessed Mother's statue on the day of our school's May procession. Our May procession was one of the greatest things we students at King of Peace did, and we did it better than any other Catholic school in the area.

For reasons I cannot explain, our processions were always held in perfect weather. It was always on a hot, sunny Sunday afternoon in May, usually on Mother's Day. We walked in long endless queues, city block after city block, in front of the May Queen, her court of ladies-in-waiting, and the large beautiful statue of the Virgin Mary. Big, muscular men always carried the large statue and during the war, many of these men were soldiers, sailors, airmen, or marines home on leave. As we processed, we sang hymns to Mary, hymns that would be burned into our memories forever. We would also recite numerous prayers.

It was all very serious and solemn because our Franciscan nuns made certain we thought of it that way. It was an opportunity for us to show our Catholic faith, devotion, manners and education to other Catholics as well as to non-Catholics.

Our processions were long and big, because every student and every church organization and society walked in the procession, including Nonna's Sacred Heart Society. It was filled with pageantry, color, costumes, and customs that were part of our Italian heritage.

The May procession was also a silently joyous time for the entire student body knew that it signaled the end of another school year. Summer vacation would soon begin!

The year Annie was May Queen was a very special and proud moment for the kids on my block who attended King of Peace. Not every neighborhood could claim to have had a celebrated May Queen from their very own street. That year all the kids on my block walked with extended chests and heads held high, like military men, proudly leading the way for our May Queen, Annie.

None was as proud I was, because I was closer to Annie—after all, she had been my tutor.

So, Annie was in my life as someone who could never do any wrong. In all the years of our friendship, she remained perfect. She was so perfect that she even married the perfect guy. In a plan that could only have been made in heaven, she married Vince, another special person to me. Vince lived directly behind us, across the alley from our house. Everyone said he looked like the movie actor John Garfield. For some unknown reason, he befriended me when I was a youngster and became like a big brother. As a young boy, I would watch him play baseball and I became interested in this sport because of him. He taught me "grown-up things" like how to play checkers, Chinese checkers, touch football, gin rummy and poker. He was always a big hero to me. The marriage of Vince to Annie made the perfect couple.

Of course, with Annie's guidance and care, I learned my grammar. Each tutoring night Annie would carefully and plainly go over sentence construction, pronunciations, parts of speech, and composition. She showed me how to diagram a sentence, now a forgotten science, but one that was helpful to me through high school and college. At the end of each half-hour lesson, she would test me. If my answers were not satisfactory, she would make me sit me down and study longer, as she did her own homework.

Many times, I would fake stupidity so that I could watch Annie do her homework. She did her written homework in ink.

Writing in ink was an honor reserved for upper grades. It was a "grown-up" thing to do. Students in the lower grades were forbidden by the sisters to write with ink. We had to use pencils with big erasers on them. Only when we reached the halfway mark in grade schooling, namely the fifth grade, were we permitted to use a fountain pen and ink.

Ink writers didn't make mistakes like I did. They didn't need to erase anything because they were so careful, so grown-up and so much smarter.

For reasons I cannot explain, I was obsessed with Annie's fountain pen. It always looked so comfortable in her hand. It glided across her lined homework paper as if the paper were a piece of satin. Often I would ask Annie if she needed to refill her pen because I loved watching her put the pen in the bottle of ink, pull the small gold tap that was on the side of the pen, and magically draw the ink into the stomach of the pen.

Annie's fountain pen was fat and black and it had a twist-off cap. The cap of the pen was the main attraction. It was cut at an angle and the surface of the flat angled side was white, in stark contrast to the rest of the pen.

I knew from the moment I saw this pen that I had to have one like it in reserve for my "ink writing" days. I embarked on a new and difficult quest to earn enough money to buy a fountain pen just like Annie's white-tipped pen.

That winter, I shoveled snow off many sidewalks and cleaned snow off a lot of cars to earn money. After saving what I thought was a large amount of money, I asked Annie to take me to the five-and-ten-cent store on Point Breeze Avenue to buy a magical fountain pen just like hers.

One bright Saturday, she and I walked to the store together. When we inquired at the school supply counter, however, the clerk informed us that the store had not had Annie's pen in stock for many, many months and that she didn't think it would ever be reordered.

I was crushed.

For three weekends in a row, I threw all obedience to the wind and took the forbidden walk to "The Lane," as Point Breeze Avenue was sometimes called, by myself, to the five-and-ten-cent store. Each time, when I was told the pen was not in stock or being reordered, my heart would break.

Finally, out of frustration and in surrender, and because I was afraid I would spend my hard-earned money on something else, I bought a plain black fountain pen that was just as magical as Annie's pen for it also held ink in its stomach; all it lacked was the white-tipped top. It was better than nothing but still I walked home totally dejected. Each step took me further from my dream of my "special pen."

When I got home, I removed my coat, scarf, gloves and hat and sat down in the living room. I took the pen in my hand and sat looking at it, wishing and wanting it to change into Annie's pen. I was so disappointed I wanted to cry, but I was a boy, and boys didn't cry.

From the kitchen, I smelled coffee and heard Nonna humming one of her Italian songs. Dragging my feet, I walked slowly through the house to the back kitchen. The closer I got, the stronger was the smell of a newly brewed pot of coffee.

"Vinzee, come! Coffee!" Nonna said, joyfully.

I looked at the kitchen table and was surprised to see it already had a setting for two, with hot steam coming from two cups of newly poured coffee.

"Cold out today, isn't it?" Nonna asked as she returned to humming her tune.

I sat in one of the chairs, put my new pen on the tabletop and slowly began preparing my coffee.

Nonna sat beside me, still humming her tune.

Suddenly she stopped.

"Oh my goodness, what a beautiful pen. Where did you get it?"

"I bought it with the money I earned shoveling and cleaning snow off of cars," I replied dully.

Nonna reached for the pen and held it in her hand like it was a precious jewel. She always had respect for things of learning, and I knew she was in awe of the pen. As she held it, it looked clumsy and uncomfortable in her hardworking hand. A pen was something she had never owned and would never use. Her instrument of writing was always a pencil because she could erase what she wrote.

She put the pen next to her cup, picked up her spoon, and began stirring her coffee.

"Today I was thinking of a story I once heard. It is one of my favorite stories. It was written by a great Italian writer whose name I cannot recall. I always liked this story. Would you like for me to tell you one of my favorite stories, Vincenzo?"

I forgot my disappointment and got excited. I always enjoyed moments like this because they allowed me to be closer with her. I nodded my head.

"Good." She inhaled the warm steam from her cup and for a few quick moments savored her coffee. Then she gently replaced the cup in the saucer with such elegance that I thought of a similar elegance acted out by an old Hollywood movie star in a motion picture I had seen. She wet her lips and her eyes sparkled. She was in her favorite role—she was a storyteller.

"When Joseph and Mary were returning home to Nazareth from Egypt after living there for many years because of Herod, they came upon this small desert village. Now we know that the journey through the desert was very bad because it was always hot and the heat makes people grow tired very quickly. The Holy Family was tired and needed to rest because of the heat, so they decided to stay the night at this small desert village.

"Now, this particular village was a very, very poor village. The houses were all very small and in need of many repairs. There were no paved streets, only dirt roads that ran through the village. There was no stream nearby, and the water well that for years had supplied the villagers with water was now dry. The villagers had to walk several miles to get water for their everyday needs.

"The young men of the village had to travel many, many miles to find work and sometimes they would be gone for days or weeks. This left the village with only women and children and a few old people.

"Joseph and Mary were sad to see how poor the villagers were, and it didn't take them too long to conclude that the villagers were poorer than they were. Even sadder, Mary and Joseph saw that many children of the village were sickly. They tried to help as best they could, but it was impossible to provide everything the people needed.

"The sickest child in the village was a beautiful baby boy around the age of Jesus. He was sick with a very bad illness that everyone knew was going to eventually kill him.

"Mary felt so sorry for this baby that she gave the baby's mother some food and clothing. Though the boy seemed to get somewhat stronger, he remained very ill and weak.

"Now as I told you, and as you most likely learned in school, the desert is without water because it rarely rains there. It is mostly sand and rocks. It had not rained in this village for many, many months.

"Mary knew this, but that night she decided to give the baby Jesus a small washing. She got a little bit of water and poured it into a very small bowl and with a damp cloth began wiping the Child Jesus' little body.

"Jesus was refreshed and became very playful. Mary was pleased. She had done a good thing. When she had finished bathing the Christ Child, she asked Joseph to hold Him and she went out of the tent that Joseph had pitched for the night to throw what little water was left in the bowl into the desert sands. Just as she was about to throw the water away, the mother of the very sick baby boy came walking by and asked Mary for the water so she could bathe her baby.

"'This water is dirty,' Mary said to the mother of the sick boy.

"'It doesn't matter,' the other mother said sadly. 'I want to bathe my son because I believe he will die tonight and I want to ready him for death.'

"Mary was filled with pity and willingly gave the water to the mother. With tears in her eyes, she turned, entered the tent, and tended to Jesus and Joseph. After Jesus had gone to sleep, Mary shared her sadness with Joseph by telling him about the mother's request. That night Mary could not sleep because she could not stop thinking about the lady and the beautiful little sick boy. Silently, she wished the water had been as clean and as good as it was when she first bathed Baby Jesus.

"Early the next morning, Joseph began preparing for

their long journey into the desert which would take them closer to Nazareth. As he was packing the Holy Family's donkey, the mother of the sick boy walked by holding her sick child's hand. The boy was walking, smiling and was very playful. He was laughing and seemed very healthy. Joseph stopped packing and looked on in total amazement. He could not believe his eyes.

"Moments later when Mary came from the tent, Joseph told her what he had seen. She was just as surprised as Joseph but happy to hear the boy had survived the night.

"As the Holy Family rode out of the village, the mother of the sick boy stopped them and showed them her happy, playful boy who had been so sick.

"'Dear mother,' Mary said to the happy mother. 'The Lord has given you a new child to raise. Praise God always.'

"'I know what has happened is a miracle,' the other mother answered. 'As soon as I bathed my son in the water you gave me he became better.'

"Joseph looked quickly at Mary. Mary glanced back and smiled and she kept this story in her heart."

Nonna rose from the table with her empty coffee cup in her hand.

"Today I saw Annie and she told me that you could not find another pen like hers. Are you disappointed by this, Vinzee?"

She turned her head to look at me.

I didn't want to answer her. The disappointment had returned again and I was afraid that if I spoke, Nonna would hear me cry.

"That is a beautiful pen you've got. It will do good things for you when you have to use it. It might not be as good as Annie's and it may be second-best, but it still will do good. Just like the water in my story. It also was second-best, but look what it did. If something second-best makes things good, then it becomes the best. Sometimes things that are second-best, besides being better than nothing, are as good as anything else for they can create miracles."

She leaned over, picked up the pen, and slipped it across the table to let it rest by my clenched fist.

"Now take good care of your pen. Treat it with respect because it is yours and only yours."

I looked down at the pen for a long time and finally picked it up, smiling. I rose from my chair and walked over to her and hugged her.

"I understand," she said. "Now go put your pen in a safe place and then go and play."

I ran from the kitchen to my room and carefully put my pen in a secret and safe place. As I was running down the steps to go outside to play, I began to wonder what happened to that little boy in Nonna's story. When I reached the bottom step and the living room I called back to Nonna in the kitchen, "Nonna what happened to the little boy who got the second-best water?"

I heard her giggle to herself and then say, "Oh, he turned out pretty good. He became the first saint to go to heaven. Some say he is the only saint that we know is in heaven besides Mary, because Jesus made him a saint. He was on Calvary with Jesus and turned out to be a good thief. His name was Dismas; he was the Good Thief."

From that day on and into high school and college, I called my pen "Dismas." I loved my "second-best" pen with its magical stomach as it glided over my papers as if they were satin.

CHAPTER FIVE

• THE DAY NONNA FORGOT GOD •

When the milkman delivered the bottles of milk in the winter months, the cream in the milk would rise and move its way up the neck of the glass bottle, pushing the small paper tab up. The result would be cream sitting on the opening of the bottle like solid ice cream.

One day, long before the war, Nonna went to the door of her house to get the early-morning milk delivery. As she reached for the neck of the glass bottle the icy cream caused her to lose her grip, and the bottle of milk slipped and broke over the front steps of the house.

From up the street came the cry of Zia Filamena, the street authority on ill fortune and bad omens. To validate her authority she was blind in one eye.

"Minnacucci! (a nickname that Nonna disliked) Leave it alone. This is a bad omen. It is the evil eye!"

Nonna froze in place as she watched this frail old woman, who was in her late nineties. Zia Filamena was perpetually in black for she had buried all of her children, her in-laws and even some of her grandchildren.

Within moments, Zia Filamena was at the bottom of the steps examining the spill.

"Oh, Minnacucci, this is bad. Someone is going to be in pain. You must do a fix tonight to ward off this bad sign."

"What do you mean, Zia Filamena? I'll just sweep it up."

"No you must get the broken glass and wrap it in paper and throw it in the furnace. The bad sign must be destroyed or pain will come to you or your family."

Nonna, always the guardian of her family and also aware of the authority of Zia Filamena, stood with her arms folded across her chest. Because she was cold without a coat or sweater on, and for reasons she could not explain, she decided to listen to this old woman.

"Tonight at midnight, you must get a big pot of water and boil it for six minutes, then throw in a whole fresh clove of garlic and a tablespoon of salt. Let it boil for six more minutes, then carry the pot to the front door and throw it on the steps. Immediately shut the door and go to bed. Call on Santa Lucia to remove the evil eye. This will chase all the evil from your house."

Looking up at Nonna, with her one good eye, she asked, "Do you understand? If not, then you will be held responsible for the harm that will come to your family."

Nonna nodded and quickly bid the old lady "*Ciao*" and went into the warmth of the house.

That night, she followed Zia Filamena's instructions and did exactly as she had been told. After throwing the water on the steps, she dropped the big pot in the kitchen sink, unclean—an act unthinkable—and hurried to bed to ask Saint Lucy to help her family.

The next morning, my Uncle Lawrence, as he left the house for work, slipped on the icy steps and sprained his ankle.

From the bottom of the steps he called his mother, who raced to the door and saw him gingerly rubbing his ankle.

From up the street Nonna heard a scratchy voice calling, "I *told* you something bad would happen."

"Old Lady, stay away from me with your crazy ideas. This happened because I listened to you and not to God. It wasn't your stupid remedy that made this happen—it was my stupidity."

By this time, my aunts had come to the door and everyone helped Uncle Lawrence into the house. "Mom, what happened?" my Aunt Rita asked.

"Yeah, Mom what was all that yelling about?" my mother asked.

"It was me yelling at that witch, Zia Filamena. What happened is that for one day, I forgot God."

CHAPTER SIX

• You Cannot Lose God •

Before the war, my Aunt Jenny's husband, Uncle Joe, became sick and was out of work for almost a year. Aunt Jenny was forced to go to work to support the family until her husband got well again. For that year, Nonna would travel every Friday afternoon to their house to help clean, wash, cook and tend to my cousins. She would stay the night and return home on Saturday.

Most of the time, Nonna would make this trip alone. This was worrisome for us because she had to take first a trolley car, then the subway, the El and finally another trolley to get to Aunt Jenny's house. Every time she left on Friday, Uncle Lawrence, Aunt Rita and my mother supplied her with money for a taxicab—all as a precaution in case she got lost. But to everyone's surprise, Nonna never got lost, despite the fact that she could not read the signs at the subway, El and trolley stops.

Occasionally, Nonna took me with her. When I went, I had to follow two strict and ironclad rules. One, I should not talk to Nonna all the way there or back, and two, I was to pray to God and our guardian angels to watch over us. Though I truly hated to take this trip, I went because it gave me a chance to see my cousins and because Nonna told me many times she really needed me with her. After a while, I realized she needed me because I knew how to dial the telephone, knew Aunt Jenny's Garfield telephone number and had memorized several addresses of people living near my aunt and uncle.

I understood why I had to pray—that was always important—and Nonna often reminded me that Jesus always prayed when He traveled and all the apostles did the same when they were spreading the word of God.

What took me so long to figure out was why I could not talk to her during a time when I wanted her to be telling me many stories. When I realized the reason for this enforced silence, I laughed and vowed I would never tell anyone in the family. It was the secret to Nonna never getting lost. The reason for the silence was very simple—Nonna was counting the station stops for the station near Aunt Jenny's house, and if we talked she would lose count.

One Friday, we left the house and made it to the Broad Street subway and the El and then onto the number 54 trolley. I had confidence that Nonna would know when to get off, so I did not stay alert; I was only sightseeing. Soon, however, I became suspicious that something was wrong because we were riding this trolley for a long, long time. Then the trolley was empty and I knew for sure we were in trouble.

The conductor came over to us and said, in a very official voice, "This is the last stop, people."

Nonna's face grew white; in Italian she said to me, "We must have missed the stop."

"I'm sorry, Mister Conductor," I said timidly, "it seems we missed our stop."

"Where did you want to get off?"

I translated for Nonna and she said quickly to me in Italian, "I don't know the street, Vinzee, just tell him it is near a furniture store."

"She doesn't know but we were going to my Aunt Jenny's house and she lives on Miller Street." I said to the conductor, ignoring Nonna's instructions.

"Oh, you really overshot your stop. Well, you can get on that trolley over there. It should be leaving in a few minutes. Tell the conductor you want Somerset and Miller Streets and he will be sure to let you off the right stop. But you will have to pay another fare."

"That's okay," I said, and then wondered if we had the money.

"What did he say, Vinzee?"

I told Nonna, and she sighed with relief. With the confidence of a queen and the courage of Saint Joan of Arc, she rose from her seat and got off the trolley.

"Stay close to me," she ordered. "Thank you for being so smart." I glowed with pride.

As we walked to the other trolley, Nonna said to me, looking straight ahead, "Do you think we will be all right? I can't imagine why I missed our stop. I never made a mistake before."

"It's okay, Nonna, as long as we know where we are going we will find it. If we get lost again, we will call Uncle Joe and he will help us," I said, not wanting her to become scared though I was scared like I never had been before in my life.

"Yes, you are right."

We boarded the new trolley, and I told the conductor where we wanted to get off. I asked him to make certain to tell us, and I made sure we sat as close to the conductor as possible, sheepishly close together.

"Don't be scared Nonna; we will be okay," I assured her.

She smiled faintly and said, to impart confidence, "God and His angels will guide and protect us, because He loves us." Clearing her throat she continued, "Are you scared?"

"A little."

"This is good. Now you remember this feeling and you will always know how it feels to be away from God. Always remember that no matter where you are, you are close to God. Even when you are far away from Him, you are near Him because you cannot lose God. He won't let you."

The trolley began to move, and we were heading back. All the way back, Nonna kept looking out the trolley window and occasionally saying, "God will guide and protect us because He loves us."

I remained silent because I guessed she was counting the stops. I just prayed.

Suddenly, we heard the conductor shout, "Somerset and Miller. Lady, Sonny, this is your stop."

"Thank you," I replied as Nonna grabbed my hand and led me to the door.

We got off the trolley and stood in the street waiting for the trolley to go on. When it had passed, Nonna burst out, "No wonder I missed our stop—the yellow and white kitchen set is gone."

"What?"

"The furniture store. I knew always to get off at this stop because there was a yellow and white wooden kitchen set in the window but they took it away and they have a living room set in the window now. Why would they do such a thing?"

"Nonna, how long have you been coming to Aunt Jenny's?"

"Six, seven months."

"Don't you think it's about time they took that kitchen set out of the window or that someone would buy it?"

She laughed.

"I guess you are right, Vinzee. But who would have wanted to buy such an ugly kitchen set?"

I didn't have an answer for that.

"It had to be Satan, but that old enemy made a mistake. It taught you a lesson, right Vinzee?"

"Yes, Nonna: You cannot lose God."

CHAPTER SEVEN

• *HEI FATTO BENE*, VINZEE •

One of the unbroken traditions we have in our family is our Sunday 1:00 P.M. dinner. It is not unique to just our family. Most, if not all, Italian families follow this custom faithfully.

When I was growing up, every Sunday the schedule was the same. Nonna would rise very early and go to 6:00 A.M. or 7:00 A.M. Mass. This Mass was attended by those who worked on Sundays—policemen, doctors, nurses, public transportation workers, etc.—and grandmothers or mothers who had to cook Sunday dinner.

The rest of the family would go to 9:00 A.M. Mass and Communion—seldom later, for in those days to receive Communion you had to fast from midnight the night before until Communion time. The earlier the Mass, the quicker you could break the fast with breakfast.

From Mass, we all went directly to Nonna's, and if you were lucky you would have coffee, bread and butter or a hard Italian roll covered with the newly cooked gravy. This was to hold you over until 1:00 P.M. dinner when homemade macaroni, meatballs, *braccioli*, sausage, and salad were served. After the meal the family would talk and enjoy each other.

After Nonna died, this 1:00 P.M. dinner was continued in an unbroken tradition by my mother and aunts. Even today, this tradition is continued in the families of Nonna's grandchildren's families.

So every Sunday my sons arrive with their families and 1:00 P.M. dinner is served. With two sons, two daughters-in-law, eight grandchildren, Aunt Rita and my wife, our house becomes overcrowded, and after the meal the same tradition of catch-up is played out.

On one particular rainy Sunday—rain on Sunday always seems so wrong—the grandkids seemed more bored than usual. I decided this was the perfect time to teach a lesson in life. We were preparing to go down to the shore for a week of togetherness and I was concerned about my grandchildren's behavior. I always worry about their behavior.

It is time you give them a lesson in certain delicacies of appreciation, I said to myself.

"You guys all seem to be getting on everyone's nerves and getting into things you should not be getting into, so suppose you all settle down and I will tell you a story." I was expecting the usual resistance, but to my surprise, it never came. They came right away and gathered around my chair.

(Let me explain that when these kids were younger, there never was any resistance. They all loved to have stories told or read to them, and when I would say it was story time, they would come running. Occasionally, I used stories to correct them, but most of the time I just told stories to get them to be still.)

Boy, they must really be bored to death! I thought to myself as they settled around me. For an instant, all eight of them reminded me of someone I knew many years ago.

Not wanting to appear superior to them and not wanting them to crane their necks, I sat on the floor with them, resting my back on the side of the sofa.

I surveyed my little audience and could not help but smile as I viewed the mixed expressions on their faces. Their expressions ranged from anticipation, excitement, and interest to boredom, weariness, and indifference.

This won't hurt, I wanted to tell them.

"Many years ago, in a forest many lands away from here, Old Man Winter decided to shake free some of his dandruff and icy clothes, and when he did this he created a big snowstorm. Many of the animals in the forest said this snowstorm was the worst they had ever seen or lived through. Many of the animals in the forest were caught off guard and were not prepared for the hardship that followed. The winter winds blew hard and long. Only the wisest small animals that had burrowed their homes deep underground were safe from the wind and cold.

"Among those smart ones was Mister Skunk, who had dug his tunnel deep under a big fat oak tree in the middle of the forest. There he lived, ate, and slept in great comfort.

"On the first day after the storm, Mister Squirrel came to the mouth of Mister Skunk's house, peeked in, and with a timid, shivery voice he asked, 'Mister Skunk, how are you doing?'

"'Very well, Mister Squirrel. Why don't you come in and rest for a moment?'

"Mister Squirrel scurried into Skunk's burrow and immediately he felt a lot warmer than he did when he was outside in the cold with no house to live in.

"When he looked around, he was shocked to see all the living space Mister Skunk had. 'Oh my, look at all the room you have! Why, you could take in a boarder and still have room.'

"'Yes, I could. You know I never thought of it,' Mister Skunk said, noticing that Mister Squirrel was still shivering. 'You know, you could move in here, if you have no place to stay.'

"'Oh I would love that. I always thought you were very kind and very wise to speak to. It would be nice to share your house.'

"'Good, then you can take that corner and I'll take this corner.'

"So Mister Squirrel moved in that day, and with him he brought all his stored walnuts and chestnuts and all the other nuts he had gathered and he crowded them into his corner.

"Just when Mister Squirrel had finished moving in, Mister Porcupine came to the door of Mister Skunk's burrow.

"'Good evening Mister Skunk,' Mister Porcupine said. 'I just happened to be passing by and was wondering how you are doing since the big storm.'

"'Oh, I'm doing well, Mister Porcupine. Why don't you step in for a few moments?'

"Quickly Mister Porcupine slipped down the hole and stood in the midst of Mister Skunk's spacious living room. 'Oh my goodness, what a big home you have, and with so much room! You are very lucky, for many of us are still sleeping outside on these bitter cold winter nights.'

"'Well, if you would like, I think we could make room for you. Mister Squirrel could sleep in that corner and I can sleep in this corner and you can sleep in the middle of the room.'

"'Oh, you are so very kind. I always said that about you. Your hospitality is very warming. I think I would love to room with you. I'll be right back,' Mister Porcupine said, as he hurried out of the burrow and into the cold night. Moments later, he returned with his summer quill coat, his spring quill coat and his autumn quill coat, and he hung them from the den's ceiling.

"So the three friends settled in and stayed warm in Mister Skunk's home. But after a few days, things began to become a bit touchy, and poor Mister Skunk realized that his kindness and hospitality were being tested.

"First, it became difficult to walk around the house without stepping on Mister Squirrel's empty nutshells, which were strewn all over the floor of the burrow. Mister Skunk could see that his home was becoming a pigsty.

"Then it became very difficult and dangerous to move around freely in the burrow because of Mister Porcupine's coats hanging from the ceiling. The quills were injuring Mister Skunk and Mister Squirrel all day long.

"Out of desperation, he called a meeting and told both of his guests to pick up after themselves and be considerate of each other. Three days passed and nothing changed, so again he called a meeting and again nothing changed. So Mister Skunk decided to take things into his own hands. That night when his guests were asleep, he slowly lifted his tail—and by morning, the den was his again."

My older grandchildren smiled politely and the younger ones looked back at me, baffled and disappointed.

"The moral of the story: Never be ungracious and inconsiderate when someone offers you kindness or hospitality. When you are in another person's home, remember that you are a guest and live accordingly."

Now they all understood, but within seconds my circle of story-listeners dispersed. It had stopped raining and they wanted to go outdoors and play. So off they went, and I was alone with my sons and daughters-in-law.

"Dad, do you know what you just did? You just wrecked everything I did all week," my oldest son, Rob, said. "I just spent all week telling my kids that animals didn't talk to each other."

"Why?"

"Because they don't."

"How do you know? Nonna said that before the tower of Babel, everything in creation, man and animals, talked to each other, which stopped with the building of the tower. But that doesn't mean the animals don't talk to each other. And besides, I'm certain that God speaks to the animals and they speak to Him every spring."

"Oh, that's it…this was one of Nonna's stories," my youngest son, Dave, said winking at his brother.

"No, it was one of my own. It was my way of helping the kids understand and appreciate hospitality, something they sometimes forget when they are in my house."

"But they act that way because they feel comfortable here," my youngest said.

"Yes, and all the more reason they should understand and appreciate hospitality. If they cannot do it with one of their own family members, how are they going to do it to strangers?"

"He's got you there, Bro," Rob said, teasing his brother.

"Coffee is out," my wife, Mary Ann, announced, and everyone rose from their chairs and walked to the dining room table.

"Good lesson, Dad," my daughter-in-law Tina said as she passed me.

"Yeah, it was great," my daughter-in-law Danielle agreed.

Left alone, I agonizingly rose from the floor. The old body was feeling its age.

As I walked into the dining room I thought to myself *Thank God for Nonna. Her stories are still somehow happening.* In my ear I heard and felt her breathe, *Hei fatto bene, Vinzee.* (You did good, Vince.)

CHAPTER EIGHT

• LIKE CHICKENS WITHOUT FEATHERS •

It was a usual Sunday.

We had gone to Mass and afterward the entire family had 1:00 P.M. dinner at Nonna's house. After our meal of home-made soup, macaroni, gravy, meat, and salad we all settled in for a quiet Sunday together. The events of the past week were recapped and told and we slipped back into each other's lives, being "family."

The dining-room table was cleared and my father, Uncle Lawrence and Uncle Joe were talking politics, sports and other things men talk about. They were waiting for dessert, which would be one of Nonna's cakes or cookies. My mother and her sister (my Aunt Jenny) and their sister-in-law, my Aunt Millie, were still in the back kitchen, washing and dry-ing the dinner dishes. Nonna was preparing a large plate of her cookies, *pizzelles* and *biscotti*, and from the kitchen came the strong aroma of newly brewed coffee. My cousins, playing or studying or reading, were scattered throughout the house.

I was in the living room, sitting on the floor between the radio console and the armchair where Aunt Rita was sitting. She and I were listening to the Sunday football game between the Chicago Bears and the Washington Redskins. Neither of us was really interested in the game, because we were Philadelphia Eagles fans, but it was football and it was some-thing we did every Sunday.

Suddenly the sportscaster's voice was gone and a serious, strange, and urgent voice came over the radio.

"We interrupt this broadcast to bring you this special news bulletin…"

It was about 2:30 P.M., Sunday, December 7, 1941. "… Pearl Harbor…War…"

Suddenly, the women forgot the dishes and quietly came to sit by their husbands in the dining room.

Nonna stayed in the back kitchen alone. Though my cousins and I did not completely understand what had happened, the sudden seriousness and suffocating stillness of the house scared us. Even the city and the whole nation seemed to have been silenced.

I went to the kitchen where my cousins Horace and Joseph had already gone. Nonna was deep, deep in prayer with tears streaming down her face. *Why is she crying? What is wrong?* We didn't know what to do.

The next day, December 8, the feast of the Immaculate Conception, the President, Franklin Delano Roosevelt, whom Nonna had already canonized a saint before this, spoke to America on the radio. In the sixty years since that broadcast, I can still hear the careful, firm, and distinct voice of that man. Even today, certain words and phrases that leaped out of the radio that day still echo in my ears.

Suddenly, we found we were living in dangerous times.

Suddenly, there were people out there—somewhere—with funny-sounding names who wanted to do us harm.

Suddenly, the world changed, and men and boys went to the enlistment stations—or were drafted.

Suddenly, gaps started to appear in families—gaps, like missing body parts, as fathers, brothers, uncles, cousins began disappearing—gone, seemingly overnight. When they returned, we saw them in a new work uniform, a work uniform that suddenly appeared everywhere. Wherever you looked, there were men and women in uniform, and these uniforms proclaimed a pride that I have never seen or heard since in America.

Soon the vacant places at every meal, the empty chairs, made people pray. An un-mussed bed, empty shoes and undisturbed clothes caused us to pray. When we walked around the house and saw the broken handle on a cabinet or heard a squeaky door open, we prayed. When we walked about the streets and saw the cracked windows, doors needing painting, doorknobs broken, we remembered and we prayed.

Soon many homes were held together with one parent and many relatives milled around with concern on their faces and in their voices. "Family" became a joint effort that extended beyond the immediate, and the entire family pulled together. We were all in the same situation. We hadn't realized this could happen to us Americans.

All our days were spent in the knowledge that our fathers, uncles, cousins, brothers, sons and friends were in constant danger of harm while we walked and moved around, living our lives and sleeping warmly and safely in our beds.

Soon the casualty and fatality lists began appearing in the newspapers.

The postman, because of the letters he brought, became a lifeline.

We lived with the lurking fear that on the other side of the doorbell or on the other end of a phone call, our lives could be changed forever. The arrival of a telegram or the sight of a uniformed officer heading to a home was a living nightmare.

It seemed there was little or nothing we could do to get our loved ones out of harm's way, and a lot of times we felt helpless. There was only One Person we could go to, and poor God was being constantly talked to and visited in His houses. We knew He was the answer, the only answer. Every day in every church, in every school, prayers were said for the armed forces.

Church-going was not just something that we should do; it was something that we needed to do. Praying became our full-time job. God forbid we should let a day go by without reminding Him of one of our vacant spots. God forbid. He might blink and lose sight of one of our loved ones.

In Nonna's house, many, many vigil candles burned day and night for those not at home. They burned and flickered to remind God of our emptiness; they became our prayers ever before Him, just in case we forgot to whisper a name or a plea or a care.

When we did get sad news, our family exploded. All of us, close and distant, were injured. Neighbors came to do what could be done. "Family" and "neighbor" took on new and different meanings to me. I had never seen so much caring before. On a large scale, I witnessed and understood Christian love and the meaning of Church.

Later, I found that not all was within Christian love, as we Italian kids were called "Mussolini's mob," "Hitler's friends," "Tojo's buddies." I could not understand this for I was an American. Many in my family, including my own father, were wearing American uniforms and fighting Mussolini, Hitler and Tojo, and that made us Americans—only.

Still later came the greater blow.

In February 1942, two months after Pearl Harbor, President Roosevelt signed a presidential order that declared all Italian-born Americans to be "enemy aliens." Now the air of suspicion slipped over our entire family life. Nonna and many family members, as well as many friends and people in our neighborhood, were now "aliens," foreigners, people from another nation.

Nonna was told to register at the post office, which she did obediently, and she was issued a registration booklet that she was to carry with her if she traveled. Her travel was restricted. Her home was open to inspection and search.

Later, we began to hear about arrests. "Aliens" and all Italians were subject to arrest and could be put in prison or, worse still, sent back to Italy.

The grown-ups in my family minimized all the rumors as nothing to worry about. They assured the youngsters that we had nothing to fear. Just like them, we were born in America.

But still, we saw and sensed the fear in their eyes and watched them whisper and speak in low, secretive voices.

One carefree day, as I was walking from school, I heard the screech of tires. When I looked up, I saw three black, well-polished cars turn the corner and speed up the street. They came to a quick stop just yards from where I was standing, and many well-dressed men jumped out of the car. They rushed into the door of a house and within seconds, a man whom everyone knew as Renzo was roughly escorted with cuffed hands out of his house and into one of the cars. Behind him came men carrying his radio, record player, records and other things hidden in a pillowcase. Quickly, efficiently, the men got into their cars and sped away.

No one ever found out what happened to Renzo because he never came back. His house remained empty for years until his son, who had served in the U.S. Navy, came home from the war. Some of the neighbors said that Renzo was a fascist and a follower of Mussolini. Others said he was a spy. But whatever his sin was, everyone believed he was safer being arrested.

This event frightened me so much that I walked home trembling.

They could come and take Nonna, I thought. *They could send her back to Italy. They could put her in prison and we would have to visit her and bring her food. Oh my God, who would cook the food for her? For us? Who would keep us all together? How would we be able to live without her? How would she be able to live without us?*

When I arrived home I raced to the back kitchen to find Nonna, and almost collided with her as she came through the door wearing her winter coat, with a scarf on her head. I knew she had just put her coat on over her housedress and apron and that she had her shopping money hidden or pinned to her apron pocket, wrapped up in a handkerchief.

"I am going to the chicken store to buy a chicken. Come with me, and when you come back, you can do your homework."

I grabbed her hand for security, but it rather quickly changed to protectiveness. Whose protection, I do not know, for at that moment I needed her and yet believed I was protecting her.

We walked together out of the house and down the street to 22nd Street and the chicken store.

As we came to the end of our city block, Minnie and Loretta, two of our neighbors, were talking in low whispers. As Nonna neared, they blurted out in Italian that Renzo had been arrested.

"It is just the beginning, Domenica. Soon we will all be deported," Minnie said in Italian.

"Deport us for what? None of us are *Fascista*." Nonna retorted. "We are old and fat house women. What did we ever do? Do you think *Facciona* [Nonna's nickname for Mussolini] would want us? What would he do with us?"

"He could kill us!" replied Minnie.

"America doesn't want us!" Loretta chimed.

"America wants us; she just forgot for a moment, and if *Facciona* killed us it would be only because we are Americans—which we are—and that would mean we were being killed like our sons and sons-in-law are being killed. We could die for America as they are dying. Is that bad?"

The two women looked at Nonna and smiled politely. I was sure they did not like her logic. Softly, they said *arrivederci* and moved away.

Nonna and I resumed walking in silence. I was basking in her courage and I was proud of her, yet I was surprised by her curtness with our neighbors. This was not like her. For an instant, I believed that she was short with them because she was tired of hearing the rumors, or maybe she said it to persuade herself.

"Oh, Vinzee, these are bad times." She looked down at me. "Are you scared of all that is happening?"

"Yes. I saw Renzo get taken out of his house."

"I'm sorry you saw that and I am sure that scared you. But many think Renzo was a friend of *Facciona* and that scared them. Today, I think everyone is scared, especially President Roosevelt and that man Hoover. When people have doubts about your friendship, they always act scared and distrustful, and they do what they have to do to protect themselves. But in time, your friendship will make them see they should trust you. All this will take time, but watch, God will make it good."

"Nonna, do you think they will ship you back?"

"To *Facciona*? The only thing I can do for him is cook for him, and after I cook him a few bad meals, he'll gladly send me home to America with hopes that I can ruin everyone's stomach here. Him and *Labbro Peloso* ["Hairy Lip," her name for Hitler] would send me back as their secret weapon. But when I would come back, I would cook the best ravioli and gnocchi supper for our boys."

"Nonna, don't joke like that. I'm trying to be serious because I am scared."

"I'm sorry," she said controlling her need to laugh at her own silliness.

"Do you know that some of the kids in the other neighborhoods are beginning to call us names? They hate us because we are Italian." I wanted her to be as disturbed as I was over the name-calling.

She became serious quickly.

"Oh, Vinzee. I am very sorry to hear this." She let go of my hand and, wrapping her arm around me, pulled me to her side as she looked down at me.

"This is bad because I can see you are angry."

"I hate them back!" I blurted out.

"Hmm. Are you very sure of that, Vincenzo? Are you sure you hate them?"

"Yes!" I was emphatic.

"That is no good because no one in our family taught you to hate. It is the devil doing this to you, so be careful and stay close to God. If not, if you let yourself go, you might be serving Satan and not God."

Having jolted me back to her way of thinking, she smiled.

"Ah, Vinzee this will pass. You wait and see, but meantime you should never be ashamed of being Italian. We are an ancient people who have learned much in living and have added much to the life of the world. Without us, art, music, songs, cooking and love would have been empty. So walk with your head high and be proud. God understands that kind of pride. Next you have to trust in God's love. I believe He will take care of all that is happening, and I believe He is permitting this to happen for a reason. First of all, when things turn bad in life, it is our opportunity to pray. So God is giving us the opportunity to pray. Remember Jesus told us to love our enemies. This is something I have been forgetting to do because *Facciona* is not a friend of the Italian people; he is only *Labbro Peloso*'s friend. You see, Jesus is testing us. It seems every so often He makes things happen so as to remind us to love."

I looked up at her face and normalcy slid back into my life.

She again grabbed my hand and together we walked briskly, proudly up the street.

"I don't think these other children hate Italians, Vinzee. Hate is a strong emotion. It is a black thing that only satisfies for a little while. A person who acts like they hate is only trying to cover up something that is missing, and that missing thing is usually love. People like that need God. So, you be happy that you love God and, above all, that God loves you. Never think hate."

Our conversation ended as we walked into the chicken store. The chicken store was one of my not-so-favorite places to go. Sawdust covered the floor and I thought that was neat because as Nonna was being waited on, I could quietly gather and scrape the sawdust with my shoes and make little mounds out of it. I also liked going there because there were live chickens clucking nervously in wooden cages. Living in the city, these were the only live farm animals I ever saw. From these cages, people picked the chicken they wanted. After it was captured by the "chicken-man," it was taken into the back, and moments later he would return with a package containing the dead chicken. I disliked the store because it stank of chickens.

Nonna quickly picked the chicken she wanted. The store-owner held the chicken by its feet and lifted it high in the air.

"A nice, fat one, Domenica, huh?" Nonna simply nodded her head.

After the chicken was all wrapped up in brown paper and put in a brown paper bag and paid for, we started home. This time we did not speak to each other for now we were facing the winter wind as it pressed against our every step.

When we arrived, I immediately hung my coat in the closet and started to do my homework. Nonna walked directly to the kitchen. Just as I got into diagramming some of my English sentences, I smelled the re-brewing of morning coffee. Distracted, I dropped my pencil and followed the tempting smell. I found Nonna standing over the porcelain table with her back to me.

"Look at this," she said.

I walked to her side and saw the plucked chicken sitting in a cooking pan. Its white skin was stretched tightly over its bony frame; it very little resembled the big, fat, feathered chicken that the chicken-man had shown us.

"This is the way we look when we have no love for God. We are naked. This is the way we look without the love of God—bare. With hope in God and the love of God we look like that big beautiful chicken back in the store." She looked at me. "So I know that God loves me and will take care of this problem we have because I know He does not want me to look like this poor sad chicken."

The war moved on like the cold winter, and the war news continued to be bad.

Guam and the Wake Islands were now in Japan's hands and we were losing the Philippines. Burma, Singapore, and the Solomon Islands had been taken by Japan. Germany had all of Western Europe and was pushing hard in Russia, and they and the Italians were fighting in North Africa. Newspapers and radios reported that the Japanese had bombed and shelled the American possessions of Baker, Howland, and the Johnston Islands. No one knew that America owned them! If nothing else, we were, as Sister Eulalia said, getting a good course in geography and history.

In June 1942, the Aleutian Islands were invaded by Japan, and the Columbia River in Washington State and Fort Stevens in Oregon were shelled by the Japanese. Things were getting closer. All around the world, people were dying. Americans of German, Italian and Japanese birth were being rounded up. Businesses, homes, and properties were being taken away from them.

Now my family became concerned but Nonna remained strong, repeating over and over, "God will make things better. I can feel His love." We began to hear of Italian Americans being arrested. Interment camps were being set up in Maryland, Montana, Oklahoma, Tennessee and Texas.

"God will make things better. I can feel His Love."

Finally, Doolittle bombed Tokyo, and the Battle of Midway was fought. The Japanese were not so invincible anymore.

"God will make things better. I can feel His Love."

In the fall of 1942, with the report of a simple statement by President Roosevelt—"I'm not worried about the Italians; they're just a bunch of opera singers"—the Italians were no longer "enemy aliens."

I remember my mother telling Nonna what Roosevelt had said, and Nonna laughing loud and long. "I knew he liked opera," she hooted at the top of her voice.

With that, Nonna was safe. And with that, the family let out a long collective sigh of relief and somehow began spending extra time with Nonna to help her and show our appreciation of her. Never did she remind us of our fears or say to us, "I told you so."

At our 1942 Christmas Eve vigil dinner, Nonna gave us a gift.

Immediately after saying grace and a prayer for our missing members, Nonna stood at the head of our *vigil de Natale* table and said, "These past two or three months were blessed months for our family, but before this you were worried and scared. Do you know why? Because you all lost sight of God's love and care, and because of this you were living a hell. Let me tell all of you something: when we die, we will not take faith or hope with us, we will take only love. If you want to know what hell would be like, remember those scary months, for hell will be like those months—without love. Hell is a kind of nakedness. In this life we have God's love around us always, but in hell we would be without it. That is the flames, that is the fire of hell; that is what will hurt us. For the first time in our lives we would be without love. So no matter what happens to you in life, especially in the months ahead of us, remember: death, injury, heartbreak are nothing if you know that God loves you."

She looked straight at me. I was taken aback, for I did not know why I was being singled out. Then she said, with a little smile on her face, "For without love we are like chickens without feathers. *Mangia bene e ringrazia Dio per l'amore* (Eat well and thank God for love)."

In my mind's eye, I saw that poor, white, featherless, loveless chicken of the year before, and I knew Nonna was right.

CHAPTER NINE

• ALL NONNAS ARE THE SAME MIRACLE •

As the war moved on, it seemed that each waking day we heard about war casualties. We lived on the brink of expectation; it could happen again and it could happen to our family. I worried the most about my father, away from the safety of home.

Down the street from us was an Italian man who had three sons. This family was always very private and quiet. When you met them they greeted you curtly and seldom smiled or stopped to converse with you.

The mother of these boys had been dead for a long time. I did not remember her and no one seemed to remember her. All I can remember about their father, Old Man Angelo, was that he always looked old and he was always coming home from his job on the railroad looking tired and sad.

The two older sons seemed to come and go, living and not living in their father's house. I don't know what they did for a living, but I guess they did something important because they always seemed nicely dressed and neat-looking.

The youngest son, Freddie, was around the house more often than the others because he was still young and in school. The first time I remember seeing him was when he was in high school. In high school, he was very active in school sports. In fact, it seemed he was on every team of every sport. I was told that he was pretty good in all of them.

Off and on, Freddie would come out and watch us, the much younger school kids, play block ball and hose or half ball, and sometimes he would come to the park or the nearby empty lot and watch us play baseball or football.

For the longest time he watched us silently, never showing signs of enthusiasm or care. One day, however, he began to care, for we saw him laugh and shake his head in disbelief. On another occasion, he took my team's side on a bad call.

Finally after months of watching, he began to "coach" us. We learned a great deal about playing ball from Freddie, and we became better players because of him.

I was the youngest member of our football team, and because I had four hands and four legs, I was all over the place. I somehow found a soft spot in Freddie's heart—or perhaps I was so offensive to his sense of the sport that he took a strong interest in helping me improve.

Then came Pearl Harbor and all three of Old Man Angelo's sons disappeared. Like so many men on our block, they just were gone, "out there," away from us.

From that day on, whenever neighbors saw Old Man Angelo, they would ask about his sons and he would report their latest whereabouts. They progressed from South Carolina, California and Georgia to Panama, Alaska and North Africa. From the inquiring neighbor, he always got the same truthful response, "Well, they are in our prayers."

I don't know if Angelo believed the neighbors or if he cared to believe because he never asked about other servicemen or gave the prayerful wish in return. In fact, I didn't even know if he believed in God because I never saw him in church. His not going to church really didn't matter to us because we knew you didn't have to believe in God to be blessed by Him. So every once in a while, when the sisters would ask us to pray for the servicemen, I would remember Old Man Angelo's three sons, especially Freddie.

A little over a year later, on a cold winter day, the neighborhood was buzzing with news that Old Man Angelo's youngest son, Freddie, had been badly wounded. Because Angelo was so quiet and so private, no one knew just how bad the wound was, but that did not stop the neighbors from stopping by the house to give Angelo food, cakes and many offers of help and prayers.

I became concerned about Freddie because of his kindness toward me in the past. Because I liked him, I prayed for him, sure that all would be well.

About five or six months later, without any fanfare or any big "hoorays," Freddie came home. He just seemed to materialize overnight. All we had heard was that he had been badly wounded and was recuperating, but soon word got around that he had lost both of his legs in the North African campaign.

In my innocence, I just did not think much about Freddie's condition, and a few days after his homecoming, as I was walking home from school on the opposite side of the street, I passed his house and saw him sitting by the front windows.

I gleefully waved at him and yelled, "Hi Freddie! How you doin'?"

He looked at me with a blank look and I realized he did not remember me. Out of politeness if for no other reason, he gave me a quick wave.

I could see his face, and it did not have the young, happy look of long ago. He was grim and sad and seemed to have gotten a lot older. I continued on home, crushed by the thought that Freddie did not remember me, although after a few moments I concluded he probably had just had a momentary lapse of memory.

The next day, coming home from school, I purposely walked by Freddie's window and again waved and said "Hello."

Freddie looked at me uncaringly and gave me another quick wave, but this time after waving he sat back in his chair behind the window curtains and disappeared.

This time, I concluded that he was probably ashamed that he had forgotten who I was the day before and was maybe embarrassed about that. That was why he retreated behind the curtains.

The next day when I passed by his window, I thought I would try and make him understand that it was okay that he forgot me, that it really wasn't that important for him to remember me—but he was not sitting by the window.

The following day I walked by Freddie's house again, but he wasn't at the window. Well, at least I couldn't see him. I began to suspect he was hiding behind the window curtains.

Finally, on the fifth day, which was a Saturday, Nonna asked me to go to the corner store for a loaf of bread. As I walked down the street, I decided to walk on Freddie's side of the street, sure that I would catch him off guard. As I did, I stood in front of his house and I caught him looking out the window. When he saw me standing there, he looked surprised and stared at me for a long time. I happily walked closer to the window, certain that again all would be fine between us. When I got beneath his window, he threw it open. I could tell he was angry.

"Why are you bothering me, kid? Can't you see I don't want to be bothered?"

"I'm sorry, Freddie, I was trying to be friendly."

"Well I don't feel like being friendly, so don't bother me. OK?"

He slammed down the window and disappeared behind the window curtains.

I lowered my head and walked home, hurt and dejected. I went into the back kitchen, dropped the bag of bread on the table and returned to the dining room, where I removed my coat and threw it carelessly on one of the brown dining-room chairs. I went directly to my bedroom to sulk. Just thinking about what had happened made me angry and resentful. After all, I was the one being nice, and I was the one that was trying to be as friendly as we were before, and I was the one that had been forgotten and was ready to forgive.

Finally I decided to find Nonna and talk to her about my problem. I found her boiling water for the small noodles called *pastina* which she would later add to her homemade chicken broth to make soup.

She looked at me and smiled. "Something is wrong? What is it?"

Without any hesitation, I began to pour out my heart to her, explaining to her how friendly Freddie and I had been and how now he didn't want to be bothered with me or didn't like me any more.

Standing and stirring the boiling *pastina,* Nonna silently listened. Then she turned and looked at me with a long unbroken stare. "Well, Vinzee, what you are doing is good, but you must remember that Frederico has been through some bad times. *Povero ragazzo.* I know you are trying to be friendly, but you must be patient and understand what the poor boy has been through. He probably is still trying to adjust to the life he has been given and has not come to understand what has happened to him. He may be angry with God, and if he is angry with God he is angry at everything, even himself. Try to understand how sad he is. For the time being, suppose you pray for him and ask God to bring your friend back to you. And please, Vinzee, give God and Frederico time. Don't be as impatient as you usually are."

Of course, she was right. Why had I not thought of going to God? He always made things right.

That night I asked God to make Freddie better.

Every night for the next two weeks I prayed. At my Sunday Mass and even at First Friday Mass, and at all my Communions, I remembered Freddie. Each day, on the way home from school, I walked by Freddie's window but I did not stop or wave. I walked by his house not to be disobedient or to push God, though I was becoming impatient, but because I wanted Freddie to know I was still there, still with him. If he stopped me, and I hoped he would, I wanted to tell him that I was praying for him and that God would make him all new again.

By the third week, which I thought was plenty of time for God to cure Freddie or for God to do something, I went back to Nonna. I expected her to see my frustration and disappointment that things had not changed, but when I walked into the back kitchen and saw her back hunched over the table, I knew that I had picked a bad time to seek her advice.

Without going any further into the kitchen, I could tell from her posture that she was making homemade spaghetti. She was working the dough, with all her weight being thrown into the kneading.

How disappointing! I had missed the best part of her making homemade macaroni dough. I loved watching her pour the flour onto the table in a big mound and then seeing her drill her hand into the center of the mound to form a large round circle. The circled flour always reminded me of the crater of a volcano I had seen in my geography book or the crater left by a bomb after it exploded, which I had seen on the newsreels at the movies.

She would break half dozen or more eggs into the crater, add a drop of milk, and with a fork begin beating the eggs. After they were all beaten and sitting in the flour crater, like yellow lava, she would pour in some flour and with her hands begin blending the eggs and flour together. Carefully, little by little she would bring in the flour from the circle. The liquid eggs disappeared, eaten up by the flour; together they became dough.

Being a perfectionist, Nonna would continue to knead the dough, adding her final and most important ingredient— love and prayer. She would knead it until she was satisfied and when that happened she would have a large mound of round dough.

I especially liked watching Nonna making macaroni because she once told one of my cousins that making home-made macaroni always reminded her of the first days of Creation. She said she imagined God being just as loving, and just as knowledgeable, just as caring, and just as patient in making the Earth from mud and water. I always had to add to what she said, and whenever I watched her making the dough I would remember the Bible saying that God looked and saw what He had done and said "*è buono.*" So it was with home-made macaroni—it was good!

My disappointment in missing this spectacle added more frustration to my existing situation, and I found I was on the verge of tears. I threw myself in one of the chairs near the table and without looking up from her kneading, Nonna said, "So what is wrong?"

"God is not answering me and neither is Freddie getting friendly."

"And how long have you been praying to God?"

"Three whole weeks," I said leaning forward with my elbows on the table and putting my chin in my hands…and then freezing in place. I had just committed the greatest crime of all crimes by putting my elbows, arms or hands on the table while she was making homemade macaroni.

Nonna ignored my sin, smiled and said. "Three weeks? *Mio Dio, quanto tempo* (Oh, my God, such a long time)."

I watched her lovingly run her hand over the mound of dough. She sprinkled more flour on the table, picked up her long wooden *spianatore* (rolling pin) and began to roll the dough into a large, round, thin sheet. Her pressure on the table made the table squeak.

I watched as the mound slowly flattened under Nonna's rolling.

As she rolled, the dough would wrap around the *spiana-tore* and she then would run her hand down it and spread the dough. Each time this happened the dough got thinner and bigger.

"Did you know that Saint Monica prayed forty years for Saint Augustine to return to God?"

"Gee, Nonna, forty years from now I'll be too old to care about Freddie."

She laughed loudly.

"Well, I hope it won't take that long and I hope you would never stop caring about Freddie."

She reached for a little more flour and threw it on the table before she continued to roll and stretch the dough.

"And tell me, when you prayed to God what did you pray for? Did you ask him to make Frederico friendly again? Or did you ask God to make you more understanding?"

"No. I asked God to give Freddie his legs back," I said innocently and then jolted to an upright position, suddenly realizing the stupidity of my prayer request.

It was then that Nonna reminded me of my earlier crime of leaning on her table by saying, "Thank you for taking your elbows off my table."

I pulled my body away from the table and put my hands in my lap. I looked at the dough wrapped around the *spianatore*.

We were silent. Finally Nonna said, "You know what, Vinzee? I just remembered a story a great Italian writer once wrote. Now that I remembered, I think Jesus wants me to tell it to you."

She reached in the table drawer and pulled out her most-used knife and expertly ran the knife down the roller, cutting the thinned dough into strips. She put some flour on the top strip so that it would not stick together and began folding the strips end to end into nice neat packages. She continued to do this until she had folded each of the five or six strips of dough. Again she tossed flour on the strips and momentarily put them aside.

"So get the cups, milk and brown sugar. Let's have some coffee."

I jumped to my feet and started running around the small kitchen getting all we would need for our coffee. I turned the jet on under the pot of morning coffee and even found a place on the crowded kitchen table for our cups.

By the time I had finished, Nonna had washed her hands, wiped them on a clean *mapeen* (dish towel), and had gotten *la ghitarra*—her spaghetti-maker—and placed it on the kitchen table.

La ghitarra (literally "the guitar") was one of Nonna's most priceless possessions. Her only brother, my uncle Tony, had given it to her. He had had it made especially for her on Ninth Street, the heart of Little Italy, and he had given it to Nonna as a gift on her first Christmas in America.

One thing must be understood about *la ghitarra*: no Italian Nonna or Italian Momma would be without one. It was part of the Italian kitchen. It was made with four thick pieces of wood that had been carefully sanded smooth. This instrument was shaped as a narrow rectangle, with the two long pieces of wood on the sides. Both the top and bottom had shorter pieces of wood. Small nails were driven into the wood on the top and at the bottom so that thin-but-strong wires could be tightly strung between the nails. The wires were carefully spaced—wide enough to make one long strand of homemade spaghetti.

Nonna picked up one of the strips of dough and put it on "the guitar." With her long wooden *spianatore*, she began rolling the dough over the wires. With all her pressure, the strips of dough were cut and pushed through the wires onto the table, and the result was spaghetti. After they were pressed and cut into spaghetti, she placed the strands on the well-floured dinette table to dry and "rest" before she put them in the boiling pot of water to cook.

I watched her in silence, knowing that she would begin her tale as soon as she had completed the all-important job of cutting the spaghetti. She was, as she often told us, "creating"—and next to prayer, creating was the thing that most pleased God. I heard her whispering and I knew she was praying to "Mary of Nazareth" who always helped her cook and even helped her become the best cook in all Italian America.

At last, having pressed all the strips through *la ghitarra*, she gathered up whatever flour was still on the table into a small pile. With her left hand, she pushed the excess flour to the edge of the table and let it fall into her waiting right hand. What she had gathered, she threw into the kitchen sink. After she washed her hands and wiped them again on the *mapeen*, she walked to the table, sat down, and let out a heavy sigh.

After she had prepared and delicately sipped a small lady-like amount of her coffee, she looked at me. I could see in her eyes the story was ready to be told.

"Many years ago, long before clocks were made or days were counted, and even before people cared about people, there was a young man who lived in Rome. He was a good man who smiled when he was happy, played with his neighbors when he had time, and was loved by all who knew him. Well one day, he was put into the Roman Army and sent far away from home to a place called Judea. Do you know who lived in that country, Vinzee?"

I nodded my head, not wanting to lose sight of what imaginations my mind was beginning to create.

"After many months of being in Judea, he and the other soldiers were traveling through the countryside when they were attacked by some bad people who did not like Romans. Can you imagine people not liking Romans? Well anyway, all the soldiers were killed except our friend, whose name was Sappio. Somehow he had been spared the knife of the enemy, but he had been wounded. After the bad people left, poor Sappio, all bloody and without water or helmet, began to walk up the rough mountains of Judea and into the empty hot desert. Of course, he was soon lost and because the sun was so strong, he began to suffer from the heat. For days and days he traveled in the desert with no food or water while the blinding sun beat down on him. Finally, because the sun was so strong and he had no sunglasses—they didn't have those things in those days—he went blind. For many more days he walked and walked in total blindness, falling and stumbling. He cried for his fake gods to let him die but they did not do that because his gods were not the True God. Then one day as he was walking, he heard the sound of someone walking quickly by—it was like a flutter.

"'Who is there?' Sappio asked, half happy because he had found someone and half scared because it could have been the enemy.

"No one answered.

"'I know you are there. I can feel you near me, but I don't know who you are.'

"Each word he spoke hurt his dry mouth and cracked his parched lips. He was hoping someone really was there and that it was not the sun making him crazy. But there was no answer. Young Sappio believed that the enemy had found him again and they were going to kill him.

"'If you are going to kill me, please do it quickly,' Sappio pleaded. 'I have suffered enough and now that I am blind, life will never be the same for me.'

"'I know you are blind.'

"Sappio was startled to hear such a kind voice.

"'What is your name, kind Sir?'

"'My name is Raphael.'

"'Are you also lost, Sir?'

"'No, just waiting to meet a Friend who has been in this desert for forty days and forty nights like you.'

"'Then He must be lost?'

"'No!' Raphael said with much certainty. 'He is never lost; we are the only ones who are lost. Here, give me your hand.'

"Our young soldier felt a gentle and kind hand on his arm. He quickly relaxed and knew he had found a friend and was in good care. 'Here is some water. Drink it slowly.' Sappio put out his hand and felt a small cup. Slowly he began to drink the cool water. It refreshed his throat. When he had finished, Raphael said, 'Here is my hand, let me lead you to a place to relax.' He led Sappio to a rock.

"'Come, sit and wait with me for my Friend,' Raphael said, 'I am sure He also would like some companionship.' Sappio did as he was asked. Finally, after all those days of suffering, he felt great comfort.

"Suddenly, he felt Raphael move and heard him say, 'Master.'

"'Ah, Raphael. It is good to see you. Please, you don't have to kneel.' Sappio knew that Raphael's Friend had arrived. The sound of the Friend's voice further soothed the soldier.

"'Master, Gabriel and Michael told me you had an unwelcome visitor.'

"'Yes, he came to see me. It is no matter; evil will visit us all at least once a day.'

"'Here is some water to quench your thirst and some food to satisfy your hunger.' Sappio had never heard such soft voices, or such respect and love between two men.

"'And you have brought me a companion.'

"'This is Sappio. A Roman soldier.'

"'...who has been lost in the desert and was made blind by the sun,' Sappio heard the Stranger say.

"'How...how did you know that Sir?' Sappio asked.

"'I know all things. Even before you came to me, I saw you and knew you.'

"'How can that be? I do not know any Jews.'

"'I am not only a Jew. I am Everyone.'

"Sappio smiled. 'Sir, you are toying with me.'

"'No, my son, I could not do that, but I am possibly not being completely open with you. Come, sit and eat with me.'

"Raphael led Sappio to a cool, shady place. The shade felt good to his sunburned skin.

"'Raphael.'

"'Yes, Master.'

"'I think you should get back and tell the others that I am well, for I have a friend with me.'

"'Yes, Master.'

"Sappio heard a flutter and felt a soft breeze touch his face.

"'Thank you, Raphael.' Sappio said.

"'He is gone.'

"'But where did he go so fast? Does he know his way back to Jerusalem?'

"'He always travels fast and everyone knows the way to Jerusalem.'

"There was silence.

"'What are you doing?' Sappio asked.

"'I just gave thanks to God for this bread. Now I am blessing it and breaking it and I am giving it to you to eat.'

"Nonna!" I said, knowing oh so well what these words meant and what was taking place. She raised her finger to her lips to hush me but I glimpsed the small smile on her lips. I hushed and held my breath, not wanting to disturb the delicate drama that was unfolding in Nonna's story. Suddenly, happily, I felt very smart for I knew the secret identity of everyone in the story whereas poor Sappio did not.

"And so Jesus and Sappio sat in the desert and ate. When they were finished and were refreshed, Jesus suggested they begin to walk. He mentioned that there was a town nearby and they would reach it shortly. So they began walking to the nearest town. On the way Jesus spoke to Sappio of His Father and the goodness of His Father and how His Father had lovingly saved Sappio so that he could live on to do other things. He reminded him that if he did nothing with his life, he would insult God. By the time they reached the nearest town, Sappio was a believer in Jesus and His Father.

"On the way into town a group of soldiers, seeing Sappio, ran out to greet him. He was a hero, they told him, for he had endured much for Rome.

"Sappio asked them to take him to the commander so that his Jewish companion would be rewarded for helping and saving him.

"But Sappio was alone.

"The soldiers believed Sappio was deceived by the sun and lack of water and food. They took him to see the army doctors who found him to be in perfect health. Because he was a hero, he was discharged and returned to Rome as a hero. Many years later, he married and had children and often told everyone of his Desert Friend."

Nonna got up from her chair and walked to the metal cabinet and took out her large aluminum pot. She went to the sink and after it was filled with water, she carried it to the gas range and turned on the gas to boil the water for the homemade macaroni.

"I bet you he became a Christian?"

"Not right away, but he was a believer for a long, long time. Many years later and long after meeting his Desert Friend, Saint Peter came to Rome. The two men met and then Sappio became a Christian."

"And he told everyone the story of finding Jesus and being with Him?"

"Yes, he told the story to many people and many people came to believe in Jesus because of his desert story."

"And because he could see again, he was a living miracle."

"But, Vinzee, he still was blind."

"What?!"

"You see, Jesus never gave him back his eyes."

"But why didn't Jesus cure him?"

" Jesus *did* cure him. He made him understand his blindness and he accepted it. He became a happy man and lived a good life and did good things in spite of being blind."

I was bewildered. I had never heard of Jesus not curing someone who was blind. Nonna smiled. She was pleased, for she had set the trap in her story and I had fallen into it.

"You see Vinzee, sometimes God does not give us what we want. He gives us what we need, and sometimes what we need is more important than what we want."

She could see I was perplexed.

"Jesus did not cure Dismas, the Good Thief. He gave him what he needed: He gave him heaven. He didn't save him from his cross. In fact, even after Dismas was given heaven he still had to suffer his cross. So it was with our friend, Sappio; Jesus gave him understanding but not his eyes. Sappio needed to see things through mercy, kindness, and love and even through disappointment and pain. He had to see life differently."

She took a long sip of her coffee.

"Ah, how nice it is to enjoy the plain things in life. Plain things make the fancy things feel less important."

She studied my face.

"I don't like that story," I said brashly.

"Because it was not what you wanted, but it is what you needed. Think of this story and think of Frederico. Now don't you think if he understood his suffering and his cross that his life could be better? Don't you see that what happened to Sappio could happen to Frederico?"

"But, Nonna, Jesus isn't here to talk to him."

"Oh no?" She smiled. "I think so."

She finished her coffee.

"Saint Paul said that we are all part of the Body of Christ. Do you know what the Body of Christ is, Vinzee?"

"The Church," I said quickly—I was so smart.

"And who is the Church?"

"The priest and nuns and brothers," I shot back, satisfied that I was still smarter.

"And Zio Antonio, Zia Maria, Tzizzie, Zio Cristoforo, Commare Rachel, Zia Giacinta." She looked at me. "And me and even you. So if we are all parts of the Body of Christ, sometimes we have to be the tongue, which means we have to talk and explain things to people for them to understand, just as Jesus spoke to Sappio and made him understand. Do you now understand the story, Vinzee?"

"I...I have to think about it," I said, stalling for time. I really wasn't that sold on the story and I didn't understand it all that well.

"Well, while you are thinking remember that God has given you a chance to do something good, Vinzee. But before you do anything, tell me what you are going to do and I will help you. Now go or our family will not eat tonight."

The conversation was over. I knew the sign.

I walked into the living room and sat mulling over and over in my mind what Nonna had said. Slowly, I began to understand the whole story.

I began thinking about what I should do, but nothing was coming to me.

From the kitchen, I heard Nonna singing and humming a folksong from Abbruzzi.

All this was too big a job for me. I'll let Nonna come up with an answer, I thought, and got my coat and hat and went out to play. For the rest of the weekend, I did not try to be friendly to Freddie because I did not know how my tongue was supposed to give him Jesus' cure.

Monday came and on my way home from school, I saw Freddie. He was sitting by his front window and it looked like he wanted to say something to me.

But when I waved, he disappeared behind his curtains.

That was all I needed. I ran home and burst into the house. The minute I went through the front door, I could smell Nonna's baking.

"Nonna. Nonna, guess what happened? I saw Freddie today. What are you baking?"

"A cake for Frederico. In my hometown, whenever you wanted to help people you always gave them something to eat. When their stomach was filled, they seem to become extra nice. So if you take the cake over his house and say something to him, it would be good. No?" Her face was beaming.

"I don't know what to say to him."

The living room radio suddenly distracted me. It was the Lone Ranger in Italian—my favorite funny show on the radio. I began to laugh.

"What is so funny?" Nonna asked.

"The Lone Ranger. It sounds so funny to hear Tonto ask, '*Come siete, Keemashabe*' and the Lone Ranger to say, '*Sto bene, Tonto.*'" ("Tonto" in Italian means to be off your rocker.)

"And why is that so funny? It is still the same thing only in a different language. *Il Ranger Solo* is still the same man only he is speaking differently. It makes no difference how he talks, just that he is doing something good."

Nonna was using her apron to wipe her already-clean hands, and I knew this was a sign she was working up to something.

"You see, Vinzee, sometimes something can be different and yet still be the same." She saw the total confusion on my face, and she smiled. "Sit, let me explain. Get the cups," she said, surprising me with the offer of coffee.

We quickly gathered up what was needed for our coffee and sat down. "Do you understand what I said before?"

"What?"

"Remember? I said something can appear different and yet still be the same. Well, let me give you an example. When I go to confession, I go into the confessional as Dominica and I come out the same. Yet I am different. Still no?"

I shook my head rapidly.

"Let me see, ah yes! When I make homemade macaroni, I use eggs and the eggs get broken and beaten and mixed and become dough. The egg is in the dough, so the egg is still an egg, only different."

"Oh now I understand," I said with great pride in my voice, and quickly added a better thought. "Just like the Eucharist. It's bread and wine but it's really the Body and Blood of Jesus."

Nonna fell back in her chair. I thought it was in relief but when she said in a low voice, "*Si, como il Eucharist,*" there was subdued surprise in her voice.

Again, I had surprised her.

She looked at me and I became confused again. She was expecting more and I didn't know what she wanted.

Finally she asked, "How's Frederico?"

"I saw him today," I said, happily. Then I lowered my head and continued, "But he didn't wave." I took a breath deep with frustration.

"He's the same," I said nonchalantly.

"And still different."

Divine Revelation!

"Nonna, I think I know what I could say to Freddie."

"And what is that?" She said with her eyes twinkling and her face beaming brightly with a smile. With much excitement and enthusiasm I blurted out, "I can tell him he could be different like the egg but he still is the same like the egg. Even if he changed, he is still Freddie and still the guy who taught me how to play ball. He could be like Sappio and do good things. I'm going to go over right now."

"No. No. You are too excited. If you go to him with all these ideas mixed together he will think you are crazy. Get your ideas together. Smooth them out. You must be very careful. Think what you are to say. Ask God to help you and then, when you are ready to go, you can take the cake to him. OK?"

She was correct. I sat and tried to calm myself. I walked

into the living room and sat down and slowly I began to rehearse what I was going to say. Sometime later, after many minutes of calm and rehearsing, I returned to the kitchen.

"Are you ready? Are you all calmed down?"

"Yeah. Do you want to hear what I'm going to say?"

"Oh, I think your guardian angel will whisper the right thing in your ears if you start thinking of Frederico and stop thinking of yourself."

So off I went.

About an hour later I returned to the kitchen and found Nonna silently praying.

"So, how did it go?"

"OK I think. He listened and smiled a lot and even thanked me for wanting to be his friend. He said nobody seemed to care about him anymore and asked me to stop and talk to him again."

"Oh thank God. I have been praying all the time you were gone and…" She stopped and looked at me. "What is wrong?"

"Well, I gave him the cake and told him you told me a story that I thought he should hear. So I told him about Sappio, and then I told him what you said about the egg. He told me that it reminded him of something he forgot. Something his Nonna told him many years ago and that now I reminded him of it. He told me I was his miracle."

"So what is wrong with that?" Nonna said, almost bursting with happiness.

"It's scary to be called a miracle. I don't know if I like it."

"But we are all miracles. Each day is a miracle and miracles are the closest things to God. That is why Jesus performed so many of them. He wanted to show us how being and doing good touched and moved and changed things around us. We are born, live and die with small miracles in between those times. All of life and living is a miracle."

"Nonna! That is exactly what Freddie said his Nonna told him!"

"What did she tell him?"

"That all life and living is a miracle. How did you know that?"

She sat up in her chair, her back pressed firmly against its back. Ever so slightly, she lifted her chin. Drawing her arms up, she folded them across her breast and said with a bright smile, "That's because all Nonnas are the same miracle."

CHAPTER TEN

• IT'S BEST SHE NOT KNOW •

One day, Nonna told my cousins and me a story about her second-oldest daughter, Jenny. She sometimes would do this to make us appreciate each other. This was an important part of her family education. She always believed that telling things about each other made her family grow close and the story would remain with us.

The story went like this:

"Tzizzie was pregnant with her second daughter, Mary, and on this one particular day she was not feeling well. I believed she was getting close to her time, so I sent for the doctor. At that time, children were delivered at home.

"It was raining very badly that night, so badly that when the doctor arrived he was wet to the skin. We gave him a shot glass of anisette and a big glass of warm wine.

"After being refreshed, he went upstairs and immediately confirmed that Tzizzie was about to have her baby. Suddenly, he discovered he had not brought his bag with him.

"'Don't worry, I'll send one of the older children to get it for you while you dry off,' I said, as I handed him a towel.

"'Minnacucci,' the doctor said, 'please make certain you send the most reliable child for the bag is very precious and expensive.'

"I left the room and went down the stairs to the living room where all of my children and Tzizzie's oldest daughter, Rachel, were silently sitting and behaving.

"'Giovanna [Aunt Jenny's real name], go to Doctor De Melio's house and tell Mrs. De Melio that you need his black bag because he has to have it for Tzizzie's baby. And when she gives it to you, you must hurry home with it and be very, very careful not to drop it or get it wet, do you understand?'

"'Yes, Mommy,' Giovanna replied, and ran for her hat and coat. As she was walking out the door, I handed her Uncle Tony's big black man's umbrella.

"'Mom, Uncle Tony would not like me using his umbrella.'

"'This time he will, because it is big enough to cover you and Doctor De Melio's bag. Now hurry and be careful.'

"Giovanna went out the door and began walking as quickly as her ten-year-old legs could carry her. She walked the seven city blocks and finally arrived at the doctor's house. Up the steps she ran and rang the doorbell. When the doctor's wife opened the door, Giovanna told her what she was there for and just as quickly, the doctor's wife brought her the black bag.

"'Giovanna, you be very careful with this bag,' the doctor's wife said. 'What is inside the bag is very precious and delicate.'

"Giovanna was so scared by this that she almost started to cry and she began to wonder why her mother had picked her to make such an important delivery. This was too much of an important job.

"With much fear she reached for the bag. Clutching it tightly in her little hands she walked slowly down the steps. Mrs. De Melio said, 'You may have to walk a little faster, Giovanna; the doctor needs the bag for the baby.'

"Giovanna held the big umbrella in her left hand and the bag in her right. She didn't want the bag to get wet so she held it up to her waist, away from the rain. The rain was so bad that her small dress got soaked almost to her waist. Within minutes, the umbrella had grown heavy and the black bag had become even heavier, painfully heavy. She moved as fast as she could, but with each step her arms were cramping.

"Finally she arrived home, near to tears from the pain.

"I was waiting for her, and when she arrived, I grabbed the umbrella, quickly closed it and put it in the umbrella stand. Without delay, I grabbed the black bag and hurried up the steps to the bedroom.

"Giovanna stood in the middle of the living room, all wet, with her arms still in the position of holding the bag waist-high with the umbrella.

"'Rachel,' she said to her cousin. 'Please help me put my arms down. They hurt so much I can't lower them.'

"Your future Commare Rachel walked to your Aunt Jenny and slowly pushed her arms down by her sides, not without pain. Uncle Tony came into the living room with a very small glass of warm wine and gave it to Giovanna.

"'Oh Uncle, are Tzizzie and the baby going to be all right?'

"'Of course, Giovanna, and it is all because of you and how careful you were carrying the black bag and all the important things in it.'

"Suddenly they heard a baby cry.

"Giovanna began to cry too. 'Oh, thank God! I was so afraid the baby would get wet.'

"Moments later, I came down the steps and walked into the living room. 'Well Rachel, you have a baby sister.' She looked at Giovanna whose arms still hurt so much that she could not reach for the small glass of warm wine. 'And you, Giovanna, you are the real hero of the night. You helped deliver the baby.'

"'Was she wet?'

"I looked at my daughter in surprise. 'Why do you want to know that?'

"'Mommy, I tried. I really, really tried, not to get her wet, but the bag was so heavy.'

"'What?...Oh I see,' I said, as I realized what she meant. 'No, Giovanna, the black bag did not get wet and the baby was safe.'

"I reached down and drew my daughter to me and hugged her. Then I walked away into the kitchen, smiling at the innocence of the child."

That was the end of the story. My cousins remained silent, but I knew this story was full of bunk. "Nonna, that is a dumb story. Everyone knows that babies don't come in doctor's bags. I know where they really come from," I said, being the smartest one there at only six years of age.

"And who told you where babies come from?"

"My mommy and daddy. I heard them talking about it one night, and one night I watched them make a baby."

"You what!?"

"Yes, and now my mommy is going to have a baby."

"Oh, mio Dio!" With a little fear in her voice Nonna asked, "What exactly did you see?"

"They were filling out the forms for the stork because we don't have an open chimney. So Mommy is going to the hospital to have the baby because they have a lot of chimneys."

A look of relief came over Nonna's face, then a wide smile. "Oh yes, Vinzee, babies come from storks. You are so smart. But you must never tell Aunt Jenny this. It is best she not know."

CHAPTER ELEVEN

• HIM AND TEA •

Knowing that God was always busy doing things like changing day into night and summer into winter, and knowing that He was saddened and worried about the war, caused me, after months of thought, to conclude that my small whispered prayers would never get to Him. He would never hear me. So I began going to the saints and asking them for help in getting God's consideration.

After all, they were "upstairs" with Him, living in the same castle with Him, and they could quickly slip Him a note under His door, or, upon seeing Him in the hallway and after a polite "good day," they could tell Him about the little kid from Philadelphia who needed some things. Or maybe, after choir practice and praise time, they could, over a cup of coffee, mention the poor kid downstairs.

This way of thinking seemed far better than sending my prayers directly to a busy God. He would have to stop doing what He was doing to try to find my small prayer in the millions and millions of other prayers people were sending Him during those turbulent days of World War II.

When I went for help to God's friends, I went to everyone I believed was in heaven. When I was having trouble speaking, I prayed to Moses; I had read in Bible history that he stuttered. When I was being chased daily up the street by my neighbor's big mean dog, I prayed to Noah, who, I supposed, had a great love of animals. And when I needed to pick up something heavy, I spoke to Samson, who I knew was stronger than Tarzan.

Of course, I could easily have substituted Justin Martyr for Moses, Francis of Assisi for Noah or Christopher for

Samson. I sometimes did, if I found one of the saints I prayed to wasn't moving fast enough.

I went to every hero or heroine, big and small, on the long list of saints of the Church. I was not prejudiced or partial to any one saint and I found that praying to the saints seemed to work because most of the things I asked for, I eventually got.

Sometimes I would double up my attack and pray to several saints at the same time for the same need, just to make certain that God got the word a little faster.

In honesty, my prayers to the saints were not novenas, nor were they the prayers I had learned in Catholic school. I had conversations with the saints because I considered them my friends. From what I had heard and read about them, they seemed to have the same problems I had. Most of them were plain and ordinary people who made as many mistakes as I did. Many of them were always in trouble like I was. Many of them, like me, weren't very smart.

After much thought, I concluded that all these things I had in common with my friends definitely made me an apprentice for sainthood. I began to believe that I too could become a saint—if I remained plain, ordinary, making mistakes and getting in trouble.

My close friendship with the saints made me comfortable enough to call them "Frank," "Tony," "Joe," "Annie," "Terri" or "Lulu." After all, isn't that how you address your friends?

Talking to them in this familiar way was my secret, however. I knew that if any grown-ups like Nonna or my mother or my nuns at school found out that my saints and I were on such a familiar, first-name basis, they would not be that pleased.

Of course, I meant no disrespect. I knew my friends knew I respected them. I imagined they were happy to be remembered by me as just plain folks, not people on cloud thrones with starry or flowery crowns on their heads.

Nonna had once told me if you have friends that you like, you should spend time learning all about them, so my saint-friends became the object of much research and study. I found books about them and spent much time reading and studying about their lives in order to get to know them better. They were my heroes and heroines. I admired them for all the good they did. But somehow, no book seemed to satisfy all my curiosity about these holy people.

In my conversations, I would ask them questions about themselves that I could not find the answers to in books. Of course, I never got any answers, so I doubled my research but the longer I looked the more frustrated I became. Then one day, I discovered something that was a little alarming, namely that many of my friends had been great writers and they had written books filled with a lot of serious and important thoughts and ideas. So they were not as dumb as I thought they were. Many of them, in fact, were highly intelligent. Suddenly my apprenticeship license seemed to be in jeopardy.

I decided to go to the smartest person I knew, my Nonna, to get some resolution to my dilemma.

One cold winter day, I found her sitting in the living room on one of our mohair armchairs with her legs extended and crossed at the ankles. She was deeply engrossed in knitting. Finding her knitting was a rare and unusual thing, because Nonna never sat down to knit or crochet during the daytime. Knitting and crocheting were always reserved for nighttime when she, my mother, and my aunts would sit together in the living room for hours, making sweaters, scarves, doilies or tablecloths while listening to the radio.

To watch them, sitting and knitting or crocheting at radio time was a delight. I enjoyed watching their needles move feverishly, weaving in and out, up and down. Their faces were serious and determined and they seemed oblivious to the entire world around them. I would listen to the radio and watch them to see what would tickle someone's sense of humor. Occasionally, a giggle or a small remark would be heard from one or all of them, but never were they distracted enough to stop.

The reason Nonna was knitting that day was because she needed to knit a baby shawl for one of our neighbors who wasn't talented enough to knit one herself. This neighbor had a niece in Scranton who had just had a baby girl.

I sat down in the opposite armchair. Out of consideration, I did not speak to her for fear that she might lose her concentration and, God forbid, drop a stitch.

I watched the yarn magically twist and fold under her quick fingers. In the short time I watched, I could see the shawl grow in length. I listened to the soft click-click of the knitting needles. They tapped out a rhythm that always made me feel warm, safe and secure. (Even years later, the tapping rhythm of any knitting needles will bring back this same feeling to me.)

I knew Nonna knew I was watching her, and I believed she was pleased that I was following instructions by not talking to her while she was doing such an important task. I felt she was laughing to herself, for she knew I was convinced that knitting was a magical thing, inspired by the Holy Ghost and guardian angels. It always amazed me how her rough hands could move so delicately, twisting and turning such soft material and producing such graceful designs and things. I just could not understand how it all happened.

After I felt my obedience and consideration had been duly noted, I decided to break my silence.

"Nonna I have a lot of questions I need answered about the saints."

"What kind of questions?" she said, not breaking the tempo of her knitting.

Having carefully planned my questions, I began my long list. I rattled them off in quick succession. I even surprised myself at how fast I said them. There must have been an edge of frustration or annoyance in my voice, because Nonna's eyebrow arched slightly, which I recognized as a bad sign.

When I had finished, she remained silent, just clicking away at her knitting. Finally, she stopped knitting and pulled some yarn from the large ball of yarn in her knitting basket to allow some slack. "Why are you sounding so annoyed?" Nonna asked calmly, though I believed she was upset by my tone of voice.

"Because I can't find or get any answers. Even when I ask the saints to tell me themselves they don't answer me. Sometimes it is so hard to understand God and His friends. I don't think they hear me, or listen to me. Maybe I have to talk to them in Latin and then they will understand me."

I was a little proud of myself for being so frank. But my pride was short-lived as Nonna looked over at me with her lips tightened just a little to let me know she was a bit displeased with me. She returned to her knitting; her pace quickened, and she said, "God and His saints are busy people."

"But somebody should know the answers. How am I supposed to believe in saints if nobody knows answers to questions like these? Maybe the saints aren't as great or as smart as people think they are."

Nonna dropped her knitting and stared at me for a long time.

I froze midway through the breath I had just inhaled.

Do it again, stupid.

"Hmm, we talk-ah," she said in broken English.

I sat stunned. When Nonna spoke to me in English, there was no doubt that I was in deep, deep trouble. Her voice had a tone that left no doubt that I had hit a live nerve. This "talk-ah" was going to be a "*maj*-ah talk-ah."

"Come-ah. We sit-ah. An-ah you eat-ah. You eat-ah summah *pizzelle*." She gathered the yarn, knitting needles and half-made shawl and walked swiftly by me into the kitchen.

I followed her, knowing I had to be very obedient because I had gotten myself in trouble, again.

Me and my big mouth!

She directed me to a chair with a pointed finger. On the table across from my designated chair she placed her half-finished baby shawl and yarn. She stabbed the knitting needle into the ball of yarn; the yarn was left on the table, dying from the wound she had inflicted. I felt sorry for the poor thing, but then I thought, *You will be getting worse, dummy!* She began moving around the kitchen getting things ready for our mid-day coffee snack. Hoping to win back a little favor, I began helping her make the preparations.

We moved around the small back kitchen automatically, neither of us speaking, even avoiding a glance at each other. We simply gathered the cups, milk, spoon, paper napkins and corn syrup in silence. When all was set, I sat.

I sat in my chair looking at my hands folded in front of me on the porcelain kitchen table, angry at my stupid self. I silently begged several saints to talk to God for me so Nonna would be kind.

I glanced at the gas range and my heart skipped a beat.

Something was drastically wrong!

Tragedy had struck the kitchen, our house, and the world! And me!

Nonna was boiling water for TEA!

"Nonna!?..." My voice was caught between shock and a question

"Yes, I know," she said in Italian, "but we have no more coffee to spare. What we have will be given to the grown-ups and the workers in the family who need it more than we do. As soon as we get our ration stamps, we will get some. For now we will be happy with tea, right?"

This was not a good sign.

The saints were not helping me now. I had been forsaken by them because I had questioned their lives and service. Now

God had turned His back on me by giving me TEA.

My heart skipped several beats. I was being punished because I had doubted them. *Oh God, I only asked a few simple innocent questions. It really wasn't that bad.*

She sat in her chair and picked up her needle and yarn to resume her knitting. For a few moments I sat watching her again. There now seemed to be no magic to the clicking, meshing, and forming. It seemed like Nonna was randomly jabbing and stabbing at the yarn.

She wet her lips.

"Saints and holy people are people just like us. They are just a little bit more aware of God. In your life and in my life, in fact in everyone's life, there is a thirsting for God. This is our job—to thirst for Him—and some people have a bigger thirst than others. So they know, love and serve God in different and stronger and bigger ways. These people are saints and there are many of them. There are many who are not yet called by the title, and there are many saints who aren't even being considered by the pope."

She glanced up from her stitching.

"These people learn how to listen and to hear God's voice telling them what to do. They do not demand, stomp their feet, or challenge God like some people."

She quickly returned to her knitting and paused, allowing me time to appreciate the correction.

"They listened to God's voice and His letters and learned what they had to do."

"Oh, Nonna, God doesn't write letters," I said scornfully. I did not want to laugh but I was on the verge of laughing, and loudly.

"Oh yes He does!" Nonna said with great conviction. "He is always sending us letters. The problem is few of us open these letters or bother to notice they are there."

She noticed my shocked expression.

"The letters and notes from God come to us in many different ways. Mary got what she was to do from an angel, and Francis from a wooden cross, Joseph from a dream, and Moses from a burning bush. Sometimes, we get His messages even from a small word or a slight nudge from a friend or maybe a whisper from a family member, maybe a Nonna. You know there was a prophet in the Old Testament who heard God in a whisper."

"That was Elijah," I said proudly, hoping for some approval from Nonna for my knowledge. *Eli and I are old friends. I liked him; he did some sharp stuff.*

"Yes, I think you are right, it was Elijah. Well anyway, that is how the saints get to know what they have to do. They listen to God in everything and find God's answers in everything."

"Do you think they knew they were doing the right thing?"

"Oh, I guess so. It is really hard to figure out what goes on in another person's life. I remember a saint once saying that God's will is like a bright light in our lives. This light just beams down from heaven, and we can walk in or out of this light. This light has no shape or form and it is our job to make it into something good or bad, to make it a blessing and not a curse."

She looked up from her knitting and tightened her lips, frowned and shook her head. I surmised she didn't totally understand what she had just said. I know I didn't understand it, and making faces was Nonna's way of acting out her own doubts.

"Ah, sometimes I forget you are young and I sometimes talk over your head. It could take me a long time to explain what I just said. Some people holier and smarter than me spend their whole lives trying to do what I just said."

She returned to her knitting, fully composed.

I was very proud of myself for I had guessed right. She didn't understand what she had repeated but, as I had learned many times, sometimes it was wiser to be humble.

"So now what was the first question?"

"When saints were on earth did you know you were saints?" I repeated my question.

"Hmm! Well most people who are great don't know it. If they know how great they are then you can be sure they will get in trouble. Every time we think ourselves great, we have to take our eyes away from Greatness and we get in trouble. Do you remember when Saint Peter walked on water? He surely must have thought he was great—but when he thought how great he was, he forgot that it was Jesus who made it all possible. So he slipped underwater and Jesus had to pull him up. Remember, Vinzee, in your scariest moments, if you call out for Jesus, you will be saved. Maybe that is why so many saints die with the name of Jesus on their lips. They are scared and even in their last moments, they have to be saved by Him."

I could tell she was pleased with herself for that one. She was doing great and she knew it. She recognized that she was on safe ground because I had asked her a question about something she was sure of and had plenty to say about.

"I heard that most saints have thought themselves to be great sinners. Look at Saint Peter. He never forgot he denied Jesus three times, or that he lost his faith when he walked to Jesus on the water. Storytellers say he cried so much for his sins that his tears made grooves down the cheeks of his face. So no, I don't think saints know they are saints. Agree? Of course."

She put her knitting back on the table. Standing up and over me, she spoke again, but the tone of her voice had a pitch to it that instantly reminded me of one of my nuns.

"You knew these things. All you had to do was sit and think them out. Listen and Think are the names of two of God's angels who are lights from heaven. Did you know that?

Well it is true. Learn to listen and think, Vinzee, and then you can be independent and free."

The water on the gas range was boiling furiously.

Nonna went over to it. I slowly walked to the kitchen sink to wash my hands—which weren't dirty—but I needed to do something.

When I returned to the table, the hot water had been poured in the cups and the brown tea was beginning to cloud and color the water. Everything I needed for my tea had been arranged so that it was in front of my place. I sat in my appointed chair, not at all pleased that it was hot tea before me. But when Nonna put the *pizzelles* in a small plate on the table, the moment was saved.

"And your next question was?"

"How did the saints know what to do to please God?" I said, chewing a *pizzelle* and savoring the anise flavor.

"This is a hard question, so let me think for a few moments."

She reached for a *pizzelle* and broke it in half by holding it in one hand and pressing it against the top of the table. As I watched her do this, I remembered her telling me that her father, Francesco, would do that. He believed that anything placed on an eating table was always placed there by God and therefore blessed by God. So now she often broke bread and other baked food with her hands on or over the table so that God would further bless what was being eaten.

I reached for my second *pizzelle* and pressed it against the table. It snapped, just as hers had. She smiled, pleased to see that I was imitating her because I had remembered what she had told me about her father.

"Well, I think I have to answer your question with two answers. A saint always knew that they were pleasing God by the stillness they had inside. There is a certain peace that only is God's peace that makes all of us know we are near Him, and He is happy with us. People smarter than I am say that when we feel this peace, it means God is resting in us. I often think about what these smart people said. Can you imagine that, Vinzee? God, with all the things He has to do, comes and rests in you. We become His place of rest, away from all the questions, all the needs, all the problems that He hears all day and all night. He gets rest inside you."

She sipped her tea and made a little face because she realized she had forgotten to add the corn syrup to sweeten the tea. She reached for the bottle and patiently held it over her cup, watching the thick, slow syrup fall into the tea. Then she picked up her spoon and began stirring the tea. Her face grew still, and I knew that she was away from me and in her own little world, probably holding on to what she had just said. Whenever this happened I tried to imitate her and sometimes became envious of her because I could not be at the same place she was. I felt left out of her world because I had not yet reached such a place.

After a long time, she shook herself out of her faraway place. She took another sip of tea and the corners of her lips pulled back. I knew she was not pleased with the beverage she was drinking. She must have forgotten we were drinking tea. I snickered at her forgetting.

She looked across the table at me. Her brown eyes locked onto mine and we both smiled. Suddenly she coughed and her face again became serious.

"The other way saints know that they are doing what God wants them to do comes from Satan."

I drew back in complete surprise. I never thought the devil would help a saint. In fact, I would have expected him to try and keep the saint in sin, but I was not in a position to disagree with Nonna.

"You see, every time we get close to God, Satan comes along and tries to destroy or detour us away from what we are doing. The devil puts things and thoughts in our way and we begin to have doubts, or fears. He distracts us. Have you noticed that every time you pray, your mind wonders away to other things, and it becomes hard to pray? Or when you try to do something good, everything goes wrong? Well, all these things are the devil's doing. He knows that when you pray, you are talking to God and he doesn't want you to get too close to God. Let me tell you something I have noticed. Whenever I want to bake a cake for someone in our family like for a birthday, I have no problems, but when I want to bake a cake for someone outside the family, like a neighbor, because I know they are sad or sick or because I just want to be good and nice to someone, I have many problems. I don't have enough flour or eggs or the oven won't work right or the cake will burn. This is all the work of Satan who doesn't want me to do anything good. So, if ever you want to know if you are doing something to please God, or if you are walking with God, pay attention. You will see Satan will try to trip you or try to stop you from doing what is right and good."

I was glad I hadn't said anything about my earlier disbelief, for now I understood what she was saying. I sipped my tea and enjoyed the soothing feeling of the warmth in my throat. She put the yarn onto her lap and returned to her knitting. Again I heard the clicking of the needles and watched the yarn wrap and hold together.

"I am older than you, Vinzee, and my memory is not as good as yours. So, what was your other question?"

"Why are all saints so smart? I read that most of them wrote important things, smart things that help people understand God. Gee, Nonna, if this is true I could never be a saint; I'm not that smart."

"Smart! We are all smart, but in different ways." Her voice was raised. I knew she was excited because her fingers began moving quickly, very quickly, and her needles were clicking together more loudly.

"God doesn't make dumb. We make dumb because we are lazy or because we don't care, but God doesn't make dumb. Just like you in school, if the good sister teaches you something and you are lazy or you don't care, you will not learn what she taught you. So whose fault is this? The good sister? No. Yours."

The clip of the knitting needles slowed back to its normal tempo.

"Some people are dumb-smart. This is hard for you to understand. What I am trying to say is that some people are not so smart in, let's say, adding and taking away, but they are smart in living life and dealing with other people or in dealing with God. That makes them very smart indeed. If we know everything in life but do not know God, we have missed the most important thing in living. Our God is Creator, Redeemer and Enlightener. He is the Maker of all things, the Savior of all things and the Guider of all things. Can you imagine what life would be without this great God of ours?"

For a minute, the click of the knitting needle was the only sound in the kitchen.

"Besides, God makes saints; we don't make saints," she said in a calmer voice. "We open our arms to God to let Him in our lives and when He comes, He changes things in us to make us saints. Do you understand this? Good."

I suddenly became aware of the ticking clock that hung on the kitchen wall. Between the tick of the clock and the click of the knitting needles, I was almost lulled to sleep. I lowered my head to the back of the chair I was sitting on and made my body slip forward, extending my short legs. I was ready...I was completely comfortable.

"I'm thinking of a story I once heard. Drink your tea, have another *pizzelle*, and I will tell it to you."

I perked up and reached for my now-cooled tea.

"Do you remember me telling you the story of Saint Francis going to the Holy Land? Well you should also remember that when he got there he became friendly with the powerful Sultan who governed the Holy Land. Because of their special friendship, Francis got permission from this Sultan to travel through the Land of Jesus undisturbed. You do remember me telling you this? Good, because my story begins just about the time Francis was beginning his travels through the Holy Land.

"He went to Jerusalem and there he saw the place where Jesus was condemned to death, where the scourging and crowning of thorns took place. And then he finally walked the streets that Jesus walked when He carried His cross. Because Francis had seen all these things, he brought back the idea of the Stations of the Cross that today hang in all our churches. All during this time, poor Francis suffered from what he saw. He lived what Jesus had suffered, and he experienced the pain and what it was like.

"Francis then traveled to Nazareth and saw the house where the Holy Family had lived. While there, he lived in the same poverty and simplicity that they did. He understood these things and understood the humility of Jesus. Finally, he went to Bethlehem and visited the many inns that turned the Holy Family away. He saw the shepherd's field and the grazing lambs, and finally the stable where Jesus was born. He wanted so much to know what it was like that cold winter night when Jesus was born, but as hard as he tried he could not learn or live what it was like. Tears came to his eyes because he wanted so much to get to know what the first Christmas was like. But it was not to be.

"Now that I retell this story, I'm beginning to think that, maybe, the devil didn't want Francis to get that close to God. Satan had stopped him from learning of this great birth.

"So, Francis prayed and prayed, and he fasted and fasted. But still, the honor of knowing the pains of the first Christmas did not come. Still he prayed and fasted, yet he never learned anything. Finally, he became totally discouraged and with great sadness he went outside of the small hut he lived in and walked into a nearby forest to stand among the trees.

"Remember, Vinzee, I once told you that Francis could talk to the birds and that he could understand them? Well this story is going to prove what I said.

"He heard the birds singing and chirping and he became filled with joy. Suddenly, he had a thought. He called to the birds and they came flocking all around him. Then he began to speak to them.

"He said to the birds, 'I know you and your ancestors have been in the world for many, many years and I know that you have traveled to many places and have seen many things of importance throughout these many years. But tell me, little ones, do you know anything about the birth of Jesus?'

"The birds began to chirp loudly and with great excitement, and they all began to talk at once. They told Francis that they had been telling the story of the birth of Jesus to each other for hundreds and hundreds of years and had been passing down the story of this great event from one generation of birds to the next.

"Francis sat listening. Tears came to his eyes as he began to live that first Christmas through the eyes and stories of the little birds.

"They described to him how Joseph and Mary had suffered through the cold night. How sad Joseph was when he could find no inn where they could rest. Mary was tired and in pain, but finally they came across this stable. It was part cave, you know, Vinzee, and it smelled bad from the farm animals. The hay was damp and cold and the wind whistled through the cave. Of course, the birds knew who Joseph and Mary were and what these holy people meant to God. All the creatures of the world knew who they were, except humans. So immediately the birds sent out messengers for help. Soon many, many birds, large and small, pretty and funny, came to help. Birds began to bring flowers to sweeten the smell of the cave. Others began to bring dry hay piece by piece, to kill the dampness. Still others began to bring dry wood for the small fire that Joseph made to warm Mary and the babe. Some of the birds fanned the fire with their wings to make it bigger and warmer. Others flew high in the sky and asked Mister Wind to ease his breathing so it would not be so cold in the cave.

"The birds told Francis of the cow and donkey that were in the cave and then of the other animals. They told him about the old hen who had not laid eggs in years, but who that night began to lay eggs to feed Joseph and Mary. They told them about the old cow who started producing milk again and finally about the other animals that came and helped keep the baby Jesus warm with their bodies and breath.

"When the birds finished their story, Francis was happy for he had finally gotten to live the birth of Christ. So you see, even a great saint like Francis wasn't so smart. And look at all those people who owned the inns or lived in Bethlehem. They were humans and were supposed to be smarter than the birds and the other animals, yet they didn't know anything about Jesus. So good Saint Francis had to learn all about the birth of Christ from the simple, stupid birds. You know most saints aren't smart. Saint Thomas Aquinas was always called the 'dumb ox.' And look at the twelve apostles; they weren't that much smarter. It took them three years and finally the miracle of the Holy Spirit to make them realize that Jesus was God. All this proves that when we have to do anything for God, God will make us smart. Most saints don't come to God smart. They get smart when they stay with God."

She sighed aloud, and pulled on the yarn. The ball of yarn rolled off her lap and onto the floor and out of the back kitchen. It continued to roll away from us into the dinette. Nonna smiled at her clumsiness and returned again to clicking her needles together to add to the shawl.

"After Francis relived the birth of Jesus, he created the first Christmas crèche. What would Christmas be without the images of cow and donkey, shepherd, Wise Men, Joseph, Mary and the baby Jesus?"

I rose from my chair and went to retrieve the ball of yarn. As I walked back, slowly I began rolling the yarn back into the ball.

"Later on in his life, we know that God blessed Francis with the crucified marks—the stigmata—and our poor friend lived with the wounds of Christ on his hands and feet, in silent agony. What a great blessing this was for so humble and so small a man. You hear what I just said, Vinzee? God always seems to pick the little ones to do His will to be His special friends. It's not the big guys with great ideas about them-selves; it is the little ones He picks. Doesn't that make you feel good?"

I nodded my head enthusiastically. "Yes, Nonna."

"Good. It should. It makes it possible for all of us to become great in God's eyes. Sure, it is nice to be great in other people's eyes. It is nice to have people use your name in respect and with honor, and a lot of people deserve it because a lot of people do good things."

"I think President Roosevelt is a great man and deserves respect," I chimed in, "and I think Churchill is another great man. I like him; he seems so jolly and nice and he talks funny."

"I think you are right. The President is a great leader, and I would like to think he does not think he is so great. But I am sure many people in authority think they are great. The important thing is what happens at the end: Just how great are they in God's eyes? Hmm, to be humble is a good and hard thing to do and live. Being important is not so great a thing because the greater you are the greater is your respon-sibility. Everyone who is of importance has a greater answer to give God than the poor and simple. I have a responsibility to God for my family. It is what God gave me to do. I will not write important things in books, and I will not be known by anyone outside of my kitchen and my family. To some, it is a poor and a simple responsibility but to me it is as great a responsibility as President Roosevelt or Mister Churchill's responsibility. But I must not have great ideas of myself, because if I do I lose sight of God and I will sink and fail, as Peter did on the Lake."

Again, Nonna lowered her knitting and looked at me.

"Oh, Vincenzo, today I think I am sounding more like a teacher than a grandmother and a friend. I am sorry."

"But Nonna, you are my teacher. You teach me a lot of good things, and you make me understand a lot of stuff that I don't learn at King of Peace from the nuns. A lot of the things you teach me, I don't see or read in books."

She reached for the ball of yarn and placed it on her lap, seeming uncomfortable. I noticed her face flushing. "Oh, Vinzee," she said, her voice fluttering and forced, "sometimes you are a blessing, an answer to prayer and good for my soul."

I watched her with surprise for I didn't think she really believed me. Then I detected her eyes filling with tears and, for an instant, wondered if I had said something stupid again. I returned quickly to my seat and watched her for a few moments.

She swallowed hard, reached for her tea and finished the contents of the cup. Whatever was wrong with her quickly disappeared as she returned in earnest to her knitting and her clicking.

Now that I had gotten all my questions answered, I decided to press my luck and give her another one.

"You know Nonna, I was wondering. When a saint meets another saint, do you think they know the other person is a saint?"

Nonna smiled. I had not fooled her. She knew I had added a question to my list, but I was sure she would answer because she was still in her comfortable storytelling mood.

"Well, I think that if Saint Francis met Saint Dominic,

Francis would think Dominic a saint and Dominic would think Francis a saint. The funny thing about saints is they always think themselves to be lesser than others. There is always someone better than they are. I believe that is humility and something we should all have and try to get." She looked directly at me with a great deal of kindness in her eyes. "There is always someone who knows a little more than we do or could do something better than we can. We should never dislike these people or envy them because they are there to help us. The important thing is to find these people and let them help us live better.

"This reminds me of another story I heard about Saint Francis. Would you like another story? Good.

"Once, many years after Saint Anthony joined the Franciscan Order, he asked his superior if he could meet Saint Francis, whom he had never seen or met. So his superior sent a letter to Francis saying that Anthony was coming to visit with him. Then he gave Anthony permission to travel to Assisi and finally meet Francis, the founder of their Order. On the way, Anthony was remembering all the good and great things he had heard about Francis. There were stories of him talking to birds and healing people and suffering much from being so sickly and fasting and disciplining his body. Above all, he had heard how Francis was a great speaker and had turned many sinners' hearts to God. As he came near Assisi, Anthony grew more excited. He knew he was going to be in the presence of greatness and he believed that Francis was a saint. He was hoping that he would hear Francis give a sermon.

"In Assisi, Francis waited with equal excitement for the arrival of Anthony. He had heard that Anthony once talked to fish and that he had healed many people and brought many converts to God. Above all, he knew that Anthony had a 'golden tongue,' that his preaching was matchless. He had heard of his hours and days at prayer and about his humility.

Francis believed that Anthony was a saint. Above all else, Francis wanted to hear him speak to the people of Assisi.

"Meantime, when all the other Franciscan friars heard of the meeting, they gathered and began praying that they might be blessed during the meeting of these two great men. They also prayed and hoped to hear these two great men give them a sermon or a teaching. The friars knew these two men were extra-special people. Many of the friars believed that both were saints.

"When the two men met, they gently approached each other, aware of the other's holiness. They were so much alike in doing the will of God, yet they were so much unlike each other. Francis was small, short and fragile; Anthony was tall, big and muscular. God was working through and in each of them. They drifted off together and sat in a hut talking about God for hours.

"At last, they left the hut and began walking among the other friars.

"After being with the friars for some time, Francis said, 'Come, Brother Anthony, let us go into Assisi and preach to the people.'

"Anthony simply smiled and said, 'Yes, dear Father Francis, let's do just that.'

"The other friars walked behind them with eager anticipation. Finally, the two saints were going to preach to the people—and to them. Francis and Anthony walked through the city of Assisi. As they walked, they smiled and waved at the townspeople. After a while, they came to the other side of the city.

"One of the friars rushed over to Francis and said, 'Father Francis, we walked with you and Brother Anthony because you said you were going to preach to the people of Assisi but all you did was walk through the town.'

"'But my dear brother friar, we *did* preach. The people saw us. They saw two poor, humble friars who are servants of

God and who are examples of His love. No words were needed. No great thoughts or clever sayings were needed. What greater sermon could we have given? What greater sermon is there?'"

Nonna stopped knitting and softly placed the yarn, unfinished shawl, and needles on the table. She collected our cups and walked to the kitchen sink and began washing the cups in sudsy water.

"So even if a saint knows that another person is a saint, it makes no difference. They know who they are before God, and that is all-important. Being a saint is not up to us, it is up to God and His Church, and in the long run, becoming a saint really isn't that important. What is important is that we live and try to be good. You should remember only that, Vinzee. You should not worry about some of the things you worry about. You should not be bothering saints with unimportant things when they are so busy helping God. In the long run, it is easier to just let things happen and have faith. If you have to know something, God will let you know. If you need help, go to books and learn, but don't expect to find all the answers there. Sometimes you learn just by listening and thinking. If you cannot find your answer, then live with what you have."

She reached for the dishtowel and began wiping the cups dry.

"Just like today, you made me think a great deal for answers to your questions. I had to think hard, and I answered you, and I learned while I was answering you with the help of God. That's what it's all about, Vinzee. We learn by any means, by any ways that are given to us by God. We can ask all the questions, but should let the answers come from God when He wants to give the answers."

She walked to the gas range and got the teapot and took it to the sink to be washed. I saw her smiling over her shoulder at me.

"Let today be an example to you of what I have said, Vinzee. You got all your answers to all your questions in a way that was not what you wanted. You got your answer the way God wanted you to get them—without coffee—with just Him and tea."

CHAPTER TWELVE

• THE GIFT OF YOU •

In America during the war, we became familiar with stories of war heroes. Newspapers and radios told of numbers of men and women who had done great and heroic things for the good of their country and democracy. We realized that many other unidentified and unsung heroes daily put their lives in the line of fire.

Perhaps one of the most outstanding stories of heroism was the story that splashed across the front pages of our local newspaper in February 1943. It was about the heroism of four Army chaplains—two Protestant ministers, a Jewish rabbi, and a Catholic priest.

Reports said that these four military chaplains had rallied and brought hope and courage to the immediate survivors of their torpedoed ship. As the ship began to sink, there were no more life jackets left. The four men of God took off their jackets and gave them to four men nearby who were next in line. Seeing that they had done all they could do, the four of them joined arms and began to pray aloud to God. As the ship began to slip into the rough, cold waters, survivors reported the four chaplains' voices still were heard offering prayers. Two or three of these chaplains had ties to Philadelphia, and all four of the city newspapers extolled their heroism on their front pages for days.

I read the newspaper reports to Nonna as she busied herself in the back kitchen.

"What a pity," she said, when I finished reading, "that the place of this great act of love could not be marked. They gave their lives with love."

I folded the newspaper and left the kitchen, returning to my geography book. I started reading about Latin American countries, thinking the incident would be soon forgotten.

I was wrong. In the days that followed, Nonna never stopped giving praise to the four chaplains. Soon, by extension, she began to praise all priests, ministers and rabbis. At every opportunity, she remembered and then reminded the entire family of all the sacrifices that men of the cloth make. She prompted us to always be respectful to these men of God.

She reminded us of the things these men had to do and renounce for the love of God and neighbor. Constantly, she drew us back to the story of the four chaplains and of their love of their fellow man, which they put above the love they had for their own lives.

One day, Nonna found my cousins and me in the dinette doing our homework. She came and sat across the table from us.

"Have you been listening to what I have been saying these past couple of days? I truly hope so. This story about the four men of God is very important for us to understand. These men are examples of complete sacrifice and unselfishness. As you go through life, look at what you can do for other people. In other people, no matter how ugly, sick or poor they are, there is God. See if there is anything that you can change or make better or different in the world. It can be anything, even a small thing, but leave a mark on this earth that you can see from heaven and that you can point back to and show God you were down here. Let Him see what you did to help shape or reshape the life He created. To do nothing, to leave nothing, to leave no mark is not living life; it is just using time," she said decisively.

"Never stop praying for people who serve God. It makes no difference if they are of your faith or not. If they are doing good, if they are bringing God to the broken, the sick and the needy and returning faith, hope and love back to God, then we should always have these servants in our prayers." I felt that she was talking not only to my cousins and me but to the rest of the family and maybe even to herself.

"To be a member of God's family, as we all are, is a blessing and a privilege. To be a servant to God's family, like priests, ministers, and rabbis, is a greater blessing and greater privilege, because God uses them to lead us to Him," Nonna said as she rose from her chair to return to the back kitchen.

As she tossed a dishtowel over her shoulder she said, "Sometimes in our darkest moments the men of God become the only light to follow."

What Nonna had said to us made a strong impression on me because I was getting ready for my First Confession and Holy Communion. A lot of what was going to take place would come from the hands of a priest.

At that time, a Catholic child received First Confession on a Saturday. The next day, Sunday, he or she would receive First Holy Communion.

The night before my First Confession, Nonna came and pulled me aside. She told me to think carefully of what I was about to do as a child of God, as a member of His Church and as a sinner. "You will get a lot of goodness from the man who gives you this Sacrament," she said. "Do not take it lightly. Remember all the sacrifices that others have made, the sacrifices that were put in place before you got to where you are."

The next day, the day of my First Confession, Nonna insisted on coming with me as I just knew she would. All the children in my class were in the church, and Sister Mary Madeline, with the help of Sister Mary Killian, lined us up along the church wall in a long single line so we could enter the confessional.

All was quiet and extremely serious and respectful.

As I stood in that line, I grew more frightened and more excited with each passing minute. As I got closer and closer to the confessional, I actually began to tremble.

Many things were racing in my head. I was confident of what I had to do for I had been carefully prepared for this sacrament. I knew all the catechism questions and answers and all the prayers that were needed to make a good confession. For days I had been getting all my sins together, running them over and over in my head, and I was ready to unload them on to the priest who was representing Jesus.

But the longer I waited, the more new questions came to me.

Suppose I am dumb enough to make a mistake? Suppose I forget some of my sins? Suppose I am so great a sinner that I will not be forgiven? Will I feel all clean and white all over after confession? Will I then know what it feels like to be a saint? If so, would Jesus come to me in a vision?

I looked around. Nonna sat in the back of the church. Even though there was a great distance between us, I could hear her praying in a low voice. I felt warmed, seeing her kneeling in prayer, for I was sure she was praying for me.

With Nonna on my side, all is going to be okay, I thought to myself.

Safety and security wrapped around me. I was in church and that always made me feel I was safe. After Confession, I would be safer—I would be near to Jesus, and I would be near-perfect in God's eyes.

But where would Satan be? Was he waiting outside ready to tempt me? Would he tempt me with something that I could not refuse? Would he show me a new sin? Make me get even, or mad or want to hurt someone? Would I be strong enough to get rid of him? What happens when I sin again? Will I feel dirty and alone, unsafe?

Finally my greatest fear, the question that bothered me so often, surfaced.

What was it like in that dark box? In that dark box, would Jesus know it's me? Suppose He thinks I'm someone else?!

My turn came. I obediently entered the confessional and was enveloped in darkness. My mind went blank.

I was alone with Jesus through His priest.

As my eyes adjusted, I saw a grayness coming from the

other side of the sliding door. Through the slats on the confessional door, small slices of sunlight dappled the box.

I heard Nonna's words: "Sometimes in our darkest moments the men of God become the only light to follow."

"Yes?" Father said softly.

"This is Vincent Iezzi, I wanted you to know that."

I heard a chuckle, "Okay, Vincent."

With faith that could only be matched by a saint—any saint—I said: "Bless me Father for I have sinned…" and on I went, each word cleansing and turning me into a clean person. Almost as soon as I started, it was over. My sweaty hands grew dry and my shaky legs grew stronger.

I came out of the big black confessional box, and Sister pointed me to the altar railing to say my penance. As I knelt there finishing the cleansing, I felt Nonna beside me.

When I finished, Nonna whispered "Vinzee, who heard your First Confession?"

"Father Wassel," I replied, in a whisper.

"Good, always remember the priest who gives you the sacraments for the first time. That way you can always pray for him for having given you the gifts of God."

"For all the sacraments?" I asked again, in a respectful whisper.

"Your first Confession and Communion and Marriage, yes, and the bishop who anoints you for Confirmation and Holy Orders. And now we must find out what priest baptized you," she answered.

"How about Extreme Unction? If I'm sick and dying, how can I do anything then?"

"You don't have to worry about that priest. God will remember him and He will bless that priest because that priest has given the gift of you back to Him."

Nonna grabbed my hand and together we rose and walked the length of the church aisle. As we walked out of the church, I realized that I would have to remember a lot of priests. Most important, I would have to always remember Nonna because she was always giving me back to Him.

CHAPTER THIRTEEN

• HOW TO PRAY •

I was home from school, sick with a cold, and I was miserable. I was missing an important test at school, which I knew I would have to take later and that would take time from my sports. I also was missing the chance to serve at a wedding and a funeral where I could expect to be tipped as much as a dollar. This was money I needed to buy gifts for Christmas.

Nonna knew these disappointments, so she gave me her cure all for all things. "Vinzee, pray for a quick healing—and for patience," she instructed me.

About an hour after she told me to pray, she came into my bedroom carrying a tray with two cups of coffee, bread and butter. She found me loudly mumbling the Our Father in a quick and monotonous rhythm.

"What are you doing?" she asked in a voice several levels above her normal tone.

"I'm praying," I answered in a surprised voice. I just could not imagine she did not know what I was doing.

"That is not praying, that is reciting. You are not even thinking about the words you are speaking."

Now I was more shocked.

This is the way we always prayed in school, and this is the prayer we were taught by the nuns. How could it be wrong?

"When you pray, Vinzee, you have to remember what you are doing. You just can't say a bunch of words. They have to have meaning and they have to come alive."

I had no idea what she was talking about, and she could tell. So she smiled as she placed the tray on my lap and carefully sat at the foot of the bed.

"When you pray, always remember to be yourself. There is nothing more important than being you when speaking to

God. God expects it from you, because He knows you best this way. He created you and expects you to be you."

"But God always knows I am praying to Him. I always begin my prayers by telling Him it is me."

"You do?" she said, controlling a laugh. "Tell me—what do you say?"

"I say: 'Hello God, this is Vincent talking to you.'"

"Ah. I see." A wide smile spread across her lips, which she covered with her hand. "Well that is a good thing to do, I guess."

I was on the good side again, so I rattled on, " And then I say my Our Fathers, Hail Marys and Glory Bes."

"Quickly? With no meaning behind them?"

I was on the bad side again.

"Well, suppose I help you learn how to pray. Suppose I tell you that the first and most important thing—besides being you—is to be honest when you pray. Being honest is most important when you pray. You cannot pretend in prayer. You have to go to God with nothing, because you are speaking to your Maker. At a blink of His eye or a snap of His finger, you could be standing before Him to be judged instead of being before Him to pray. So keep this in mind when you pray. Remember, you are before your God who is the Great Listener because He loves you and He wants to hear you. Next thing of importance is that no matter what you are praying for, you thank Him. Thank Him for all the good things you have and then thank Him for listening. Finally, ask Him for help or give Him your request."

"But my way is the way the nuns taught me to pray. Is there something wrong with it?"

"No. You can say all the Our Fathers you want, but just say it as you and not spitting it out. There are words in the Our Father that should have special meaning to you. Those words are the words that give the prayer meaning and God knows that it is from you."

She looked at me for a long time then reached for her cup of coffee. She took a sip from her cup and then said, "Let me tell you a small story."

I held my cup close to my face, enjoying the warmth. I was ready to have her take me wherever she was going.

"A few days after He created the world and He rested, God came down and walked on the earth to see if everything He did was working well. As He walked through a small part of the forest He came across a squirrel who became very excited and happy to see God. The small squirrel ran over to God and began to jump up and down.

"'I want to thank you, God, for giving me all these nuts to eat. Nuts are my daily food,' the small squirrel said excitedly. 'And I will always thank you for this.'

"God smiled and gave Squirrel a promise that he would always have his wish.

"Walking farther into the forest, God came to the edge of the ocean. Just as He reached the shores, a small otter leaped out of the water. Standing before God he said, 'O God I want to thank you for not making me a land animal, for I am happy in the water. If I lived on land I would have been attracted to all the other animals and would have eaten all their food. I will always thank you for this gift you have given me.'

"God smiled and gave Otter his wish.

"As God turned he saw a raccoon standing by a bush. The raccoon walked slowly over to God and said in a small, humble voice, 'I also am thankful to you, God, for you have made me a land animal and not a water animal. I don't like the water much, but I guess I am not as good as my brother, the otter. I am a little robber and I steal many things, but I want to ask your forgiveness always for being an intruder. I promise never to hate those who intrude on me, and I will always be thankful to you.'

"God smiled and gave Raccoon his wish.

"Continuing on through the forest, God came across a kangaroo, who, when he saw God, came bouncing over to Him. 'Oh God you have been very good to me. You have made me able to jump high and fast and this has saved me many times from being captured and eaten. I want to thank you always,' Kangaroo said, with his big dark eyes tearing up.

"God smiled at Kangaroo and gave him his wish."

Nonna rose from the bed, put her empty cup on the bureau and began pulling at the corners of the bedspread to straighten out the wrinkles she had made.

"So you see how our animal friends were themselves and each was honest and each thanked God for what he had. Squirrel thanked God for his nuts—his 'daily bread.' Raccoon asked God to forgive him for intruding, which are his 'trespasses.' Otter thanked God for not 'leading him into temptation,' and Kangaroo thanked God for delivering him 'from evil.'"

I looked at her, stunned at her storytelling skill. I was in awe of her and could not imagine how she did this time and time again.

"And so each of our brothers got his wish from God."

"What wish? I don't remember them asking for anything."

"Oh, yes they did. They each said they would be thankful to God, so God made certain they kept this promise. That is why every time you see a squirrel standing still, or a raccoon, otter or a kangaroo, they always have their front paws in front of them, ready to say a prayer."

That day, I learned how to pray.

CHAPTER FOURTEEN

• God Will See to It •

One of the best things I remember about my neighborhood was how different, and yet how alike, we all were.

Most of my neighbors were Italian, but they also were other nationalities such as Irish, Polish, English and German, both black and white. Most of us were Catholic, but a minority were Protestants and Jews.

It seemed to matter little what you believed or what customs you followed or what you liked or disliked, or what you looked like. When a neighbor was in need, everyone on the street pulled together to help. It was as if all the grown-ups had gotten together at a big powwow and decided that they would protect each other. Whatever differences the grown-ups had, and I am sure there were differences, we kids never saw them.

Now when I think of it, I am sure this concern and care for each other was because we were all in the same position. We were all struggling to survive, struggling to eke out a life for ourselves, struggling to keep it all together.

Working together and helping each other eased the burden somewhat. Feeling another's pain and filling in the empty spaces was the wisest way to survive. Being nice to each other was an insurance against being alone when help was needed. It made things so much easier to get along.

It would be easy to say that this all happened because of the war, when everyone had the same fears and worries, but that would not be the truth. My neighbors were this way before the war and remained this way after the war.

As a result of this connectedness, all the kids in the neighborhood had many eyes watching them and caring for them.

If we did anything wrong, it was reported. We were tended to with the simplest form of punishment at home—a beating.

Needless to say, this protection that the grownups showed to each other rubbed off on the youngsters in the neighborhood. This meant that the underdog, the weakling, the "different" kid, was tended to with a bit of extra care.

On our block, we had two young people who were just a little "different."

The boy's name was Buddy. Buddy was hyper and very nervous. He paced a great deal, and he had a habit of wringing his hands together as if washing them. He was never violent or mean; in fact he was the gentlest person I knew.

Buddy always stayed close to home. Often he would stand on the top step of his house and just look up and down the street. He was friendly enough, greeting everyone passing. On some occasions, he would walk from one corner of the street to the other corner. Never would he walk outside the block without a parent or one of his siblings. When he took these walks, he greeted everyone and would ask how they were doing. If someone was sick, he would ask how the sick person was feeling.

Buddy came from a large family of several sisters and one younger brother. All of them put a lot of time and energy into watching, caring and attending to him.

In another family, there was a girl named Cathy. She was confined to a wheelchair and had difficulty speaking and controlling her head. Her hands and legs were twisted. It was easy to see that she would have a great deal of difficulty doing even the simplest thing for herself. Her mother and other members of the family constantly tended to Cathy.

On winter days, she would sit by the window looking out. If she saw you and could get your attention with a tap on the window, you would see her big smile and quick wave.

In the summertime her mother would put her on the front steps or put her in her wooden wheelchair near the side of the front steps. With all her problems, Cathy was one of the happiest and most pleasant people on the block, and she could hold long conversation about many things. To top it off, she had the widest smile ever made by God.

I remember many nice and ordinary things about these two people, but the one thing that I remember the most is that they were very afraid of lightning and thunder. Every time we had lightning and thunder—two things that I happened to love—I would think of them and wonder how frightened they were. I would pray that God would make things easy for them.

Buddy and Cathy were never ridiculed, disrespected or made fun of by anyone in the neighborhood. It just never, ever crossed our minds to do such a thing. In fact, they were so much a part of our neighborhood that we kids would often go out of our way to talk to them and help them if they needed any help.

One boy would go out of his way to ask Buddy or Cathy questions about school, although they were not schooled that much. He accepted whatever answer they gave him with much amazement and excitement. Whatever answers they gave this boy surely did not help him with his homework, but it made Buddy and Cathy feel good about themselves, especially when he thanked them in a big way. And, of course, it made the boy feel good to know he had made them feel important.

One hot summer day, something happened that changed both Buddy and Cathy. They were outside enjoying the warm sun and the tender summer breezes. Cathy was sitting on the front steps of her house and Buddy was standing on the top step of his house. He decided to go down the street to talk to Cathy, which was something he did often.

Something one of them said must have been funny because they began to laugh loudly. Their delight intensified their peculiarities. Cathy began swaying in her wheelchair and Buddy began pacing back and forth.

Just as they got loudest, Nonna and I came walking down the street from our corner butcher's store. Nonna smiled when she noticed the laughter between Cathy and Buddy.

Coming up the opposite end of our street was a group of people who did not live on our street, two young girls, a boy in his teens, and a woman about thirty-five years of age. For some reason, the group stopped and began making fun of Buddy and Cathy. They imitated Cathy's twisted hands and legs and Buddy's wringing hand motions.

Instantaneously, Buddy and Cathy fell silent and shrank back. They looked lost. They had no idea what they were supposed to do, how to handle this mockery. It was strange to them; they had never before experienced it.

One of our neighbors, who happened to be sitting by her window, immediately ran to the front door of her home and began shouting at the strangers. Nonna flew into action as well. She threw the heavy grocery bags into my arms and strode up the street. I had never seen her move so quickly. Never before had I seen such anger and horror on her face.

Nonna ran to Cathy and Buddy and gathered them to her as she confronted the strangers with loud condemnations. I had never heard her voice so loud or her poor English so nearly perfect.

Other neighbors, hearing the commotion, came to their doors and began shouting at the strangers as well.

The strangers stood their ground. They shouted back disrespectfully, arguing with the all the neighbors. Soon, however, they realized they were outnumbered and losing the shouting contest. They began to edge away, but not before one of them shouted, "Hitler's got de right idear. Dey oughtah kill people like dem two imbeciles."

The tormenters began calling Nonna and some neighbors "Fascist Eye-talians" and "Nazis" and "Hitler's friends."

Their name-calling didn't seem to bother the grown-ups, but it bothered me. I had never thought of my family or neighbors as being these things. We were Americans living in Italian, German, Polish, Irish, and Jewish ways.

Even more neighbors came out with brooms and rolled-up newspapers and it looked like a physical confrontation was about to start. It never came to that for the strangers were now in full gallop. They were running away from our street, but not without some last-minute mockery and more curses.

They left behind two broken souls. What had been ordinary had now become different. For the first time, Buddy and Cathy were aware of this difference.

Cathy was crying and Buddy was stuttering and shouting.

Nonna, in her guardian angel role, ushered the confused Cathy and Buddy to their homes, where the two hurt and now "different" people were comforted away from more unpleasantness.

The neighbors stood on their steps, on the sidewalk and in the street talking and trying to settle down after the altercation. I stood straining to hold the heavy grocery bags in my arms, stupefied by a scene that felt like a World War II battlefield.

Finally, unable to hold the bags, I put them down on a neighbor's front steps and let my strained arms fall to my sides with relief.

When Nonna returned to me, her face was etched with anger, deep pain and sadness. I couldn't tell which was the most severe.

She scooped up the grocery bags and said roughly, "Vincenzo. Home."

There was no need for anything further to be said. I quickly walked beside her, filled with a mixture of pride at what she had done and confusion as to what had happened. I had never seen my Nonna or my neighbors get so hostile. I had never been accused of not being American, and I did not like the bad feelings I was having.

Without saying a word, Nonna walked non-stop through the living room, dining room and dinette, into the back kitchen. She violently ripped open the brown bags to begin putting the groceries away.

When she had finished opening and slamming cabinet doors and drawers she sat down at the porcelain-top table and folded her hands as if she were in prayer.

Finally she looked up and pointed at me. Moving her wrist and finger up and down she said, "Vincenzo, make certain you understand this: If I ever hear or see you being that unkind or making fun of any other child of God, I will break your face."

I stood mute. I was unsure if I had done anything wrong or if I should have done something more. One thing I knew—she was not kidding around. When Nonna or any Italian woman said she would "break your face," that meant you were looking into the face of death.

Nothing more was said to me for the rest of the day or the next morning. By the next afternoon when I came home from school, I found Nonna in the back kitchen as usual. "How are Buddy and Cathy?" she asked, without raising her head from the beans she was stripping from their pods.

"I don't know. They haven't been outside since the other day."

"Poor babies."

"I think their feelings were hurt and they are ashamed," I said, unsure if I should venture a guess.

"Ashamed? Why should they be ashamed? Those other people—those strangers—should be ashamed, not those poor children. People who go around making fun of other people are hiding a lot of things in their own lives."

She wiped her hands on her apron and took the beans to the kitchen sink and began running water over them.

"We should never make fun of people who are different. It is wrong. Seriously wrong."

When the pot was filled with water, she left the beans in the water to soak and returned to the table. She tore open a brown bag that contained ears of corn and began to strip the corn with great vengeance.

I could tell she was still angry at those strangers.

"I'll have to go and see Buddy's and Cathy's mothers soon and see if there is something I can do," she said thoughtfully. "This is something for grown-ups to take care of, Vinzee, so don't become too bothered by what happened."

I sat watching her strip the corn.

"They are not ashamed, Vinzee. I think they are hurt because those people made them feel different when they made fun of them."

"Nonna why did God make them different? Why couldn't He make us all the same?"

"And that would do what? If God made us all the same we would be nothing but walking and breathing mirrors, that's all."

She walked to the icebox and returned with the bottle of milk and placed it on the kitchen table. She turned, and when she passed the gas range, she turned up the jet under the morning coffeepot. Then she turned to gather the things we would need for our afternoon coffee.

"I need some coffee. Would you like some?" she said, with a smile on her face.

I smiled back, because I knew she could never have coffee without me.

Several sips of the coffee later, when we were settled, Nonna said, "If God made us all the same, there would be no differences. If there were no differences, we would never learn."

I looked at her, completely baffled.

"What are we supposed to learn?"

"Well, it gives us a chance to learn goodness. The smart and healthy help the not-so-smart and the not-so-healthy. The rich help the poor and the poor help the rich by making them get richer."

She smiled, because she had said something that she thought was funny.

"God made us different so that each of us would see Him differently. A man sees God differently than a woman does and a little child sees God differently than a grown-up does. Different people in the world also see God in different ways. Because we see God in different ways, God uses us differently but always with the same love."

"Nonna, Sister Mary Clara told my class that we are all the same to God."

"Yes, we are all His children, but He made us different and He expects different things from us. If you are smart, He expects you to be smart. If you have a good voice, then He expects you to be a singer. If you are religious, He expects you to love and obey Him. Do you see what I mean?"

"I think so," I said, with some doubt, because for the first time in my life I found myself faced with a dilemma of having to choose between my Nonna and my nun and I wanted them both to be right.

She slowly put her hand to her lips, trying to find another example for me to understand better. "Look at the birds of the world. They are all different because they each have something different to do. They do things differently, they sing and chirp differently, yet God loves them all."

Believing she had clarified my confusion, she took a long sip of coffee. After putting her cup back on its saucer, she reached for her paper napkin and gently wiped her lips.

"Being different sometimes is not an easy thing. There is always the chance of being made fun of and the chance of being pushed back. When I was a little girl in Abruzzi, there was a boy who had become ill as a young boy. Because of his illness, he was blind. You know what? He saw things I never could see. I remember him telling me how he "saw" our small church. The way he described it was far prettier then what it was. I lied and told him he was correct; our small church looked just like he described. It made him happy, and I felt good seeing him happy. It was a lie, but God understood why I made the lie. I remember he could see with his hands by touching things. He was also a great storyteller and we shared many stories together. He and I were friends but not everyone in my village liked him. Many ignored him and pretended he was not there and some of the town folks made fun of him. Do you have any friends in your class that are like that, Vinzee? Of course, you do. We all meet people like that, but I hope you will never be unkind or make fun of people who are different. Before people make fun of other people, they should look at themselves. If anyone is different, it is because God made them that way. He had His reasons. He made them different for a purpose."

"But why?" I said, before I could stop myself.

She snapped her head up, realizing that she had talked over my head. I got a small smile.

"Let me tell you a story and then maybe you will understand better."

Immediately the world ceased to be, and the only thing that existed was my blank mind and Nonna, about to draw pictures in my mind.

She wet her lips, took a tiny sip of her coffee, and began:

"After God made the stars and the moon and the sun, He made the plants and trees. Finally, He made the animals. Now, because God had the whole day to make these animals, He spent a lot of time being very creative and different. He made the big elephant and the tall giraffe and the many spotted and striped animals. He made furry and not-so-furry animals. He made animals that stalked and those who leaped and jumped. He made fast and slow animals. Some animals were beautiful and some were not. Some animals roared and others crowed and chirped. Still others howled.

"When He finally finished making all the animals, He set them free into the forest and jungles and they began to fill the world with sounds and noises. By the end of the day, all the animals were in place and all had been given their place in creation. But there was one animal that did not make any sounds and that was because God could not decide what sound it should make.

"This animal thought that God had not given him a sound because he was perfect, that he was the most beautiful, the most perfect of all creatures. He believed his silence was further proof that he was beautiful because he did not have to draw any attention to himself.

"This animal pranced around the world so sure of himself, and then one day he came upon a big elephant.

"'Oh my, you look so funny with those big flapping ears. You look like you can fly away with them.'

"'But I can hear all the things in the world,' the big elephant said.

"'All the sounds in the world are nothing but noise. And tell me, what are you supposed to do with that big, long, funny-looking nose? Smell everything in the world?' The elephant got mad and chased him away and told him he would never consider him to be his friend.

"'Who cares?' the animal said. 'I'm perfect!'

"The animal continued to walk around the world, and finally came upon a tall giraffe. 'Oh my, you look so stupid with those skinny, bony legs and that long, endless neck.'

"'But I can see things that you cannot see,' the Giraffe said.

"'And what are you supposed to do with that long, fat tongue? Lick up everything I cannot?' This made the giraffe mad at him and he chased him away and told him they could never be friends. However, this did not bother the animal because he knew he was perfect.

"'The animal continued to go through the jungle and forest, making fun of the snake because he had no legs, the sloth because he was so slow, the pelican because he had a big jaw, and the kangaroo because his stomach was a suitcase. They all chased this animal away and said he would be their enemy. But he did not care, for he was perfect.

"Finally the animal came to the King of the Beasts, and he began to make fun of all the hair the lion had around his head and his long whiskers. 'You need a haircut and a shave,' the criticizing animal said.

"The King of the Beasts looked at him and said, 'You and I will be mortal enemies for all time and I will ask God to make certain to give you a noise that all the animals in His Kingdom will know and despise.'

"The animal pranced away, 'That will never happen, Mister Lion, for I am perfect and that is why God did not give me a sound.'

"For hours, God had been watching this animal making fun of His creatures. He was not at all pleased, so He decided to teach the animal a lesson.

The next day, the animal came across a clear pond. He walked over to it and looked into the pond and saw a reflection of himself. But, never having seen himself, he did not know it was himself he was seeing.

"The animal reflecting from the pond looked like a dog but his ears were too round. The hair around his head was too short for this animal to be a lion. He was spotted like a leopard but he was too small to be a leopard. His body sloped back from big shoulders to small hind legs. He looked at his own reflection for a long time. Finally, he said, 'Animal, you are the funniest-looking animal I ever saw. You look like you were made up of a little of everything.'

"The more he looked, the funnier he found this animal to be. Soon he began to laugh and laugh and laugh.

"Suddenly, the heavens parted and God's voice was heard throughout creation, 'Animal, you have made the sound by which others will recognize you, and you have condemned yourself to laugh for all time.' So that is why, to this day, the hyena laughs," Nonna said.

My mouth dropped open in surprise.

She stopped and looked at me. Then, leaning over close to me, as if to tell me the biggest secret in the world, she said, "Those people who were making fun of Buddy and Cathy were making fun of God's creation. In time, and we may not see it, you can be sure the last laugh will be on them. God will see to it."

On that day I learned that different was a blessing and making fun was a dangerous thing.

CHAPTER FIFTEEN

• THE GIFT FOR HANUKKAH •

Nonna had things in her life that were more precious than anything else, and she continued to hold on to these things with all the strength that God would permit her to have. Often, to help her family understand just how important these belongings were to her, she would tell stories that added more importance to these precious articles.

I think she told these stories with the hopes of getting us to be more respectful of her belongings. I also think she told these stories about these possessions to distract us from noticing her weakness for things of the world. Also, she wanted to remind us often that all possessions are temporary and within the beck and call of God.

The memory she had of her loved ones who had been called back to God was the one thing that she knew neither God nor any human being could take from her. These people were gifts from God and she knew God never completely took back a gift.

I have often mentioned Nonna's dining-room table and all its vigil lights and candles, but let me explain it further.

The burning of candles was a solemn, serious and prayerful act for Nonna. The closest thing to a church was Nonna's dining-room table. There were times in the cold of winter that the dining room, because of all those candles, was the second-warmest room in the house.

In past times, when we passed a church we would always make a small cross on our foreheads. If we were wearing a hat, we would tip it to show respect and remembrance of Jesus in the church. As when passing a church, when any of us passed the dining-room table, we were reminded for whom the candles were burning. Upon remembering, we would say a quick prayer. Many times, an image of that person would pop into our minds and this simple fact of remembering became a prayer.

The burning candles were not only for those in the war or for those out of the house during a bad rain or snowstorm; they were for those traveling, those sick, those looking for work, those pregnant or in the hospital.

Often, a larger candle would appear, and this signified the anniversary of a deceased member of our family. As soon as any of us saw this candle we recalled the date and ran the names of the dead through our minds.

Just in case we did not remember whose anniversary it was, Nonna would always remind us as we entered the back kitchen, "Today is twenty-eight years your grandfather died," or "Great-Grandmom Martino's anniversary is today" or simply, "Today is the day Danny, Commare Mary's son, was killed in the war."

Walking past the dining-room table as often as she did, and as often as the rest of us did, meant a lot of prayers were said for all those who had a candle burning for them.

This pleased Nonna, for this was her plan. She always said, "If they are before God, then they will pray for us, and if they are not, then God will be reminded of our hurt. He will check His records and see if it is time for them to join Him."

Her *ghitarra*—the instrument on which she made home-made macaroni—was given to her by my great-uncle Tony, her brother, on her first Christmas in America, and she cherished it. I remember her cleaning the *ghitarra* with careful precision and then easing it into an old but dazzlingly clean white pillowcase before placing it on the overhead shelf in the closet. I also can remember her every so often reminding her brother that she still had the *ghitarra* and thanking him. There were times I know Uncle Tony wanted to tell her that she had thanked him enough, but he knew how grateful and appreciative she was so he just smiled and said nothing. To show the importance of the *ghitarra*, Nonna once told this story.

"There was a little angel named Perdente who was always busy playing instead of doing his chores. As a result, he was forever losing or misplacing things. On a cold winter night, Perdente misplaced a star and because of this, the Archangel Gabriel punished him by not promoting him to the role of guardian angel; he kept him as a cherub for another two years. On a warm summer day, just as those two years of punishment were up, the little angel misplaced a cloud, so again Gabriel punished him. On a clear spring night, just as his second two years of punishment came to an end, Perdente was flying around the heavens dodging planets and spinning stars and jumping on clouds when he heard a small baby crying and crying. The poor baby was colicky and Perdente felt sorry for him. He took his harp, flew down to earth, and played on his harp and hummed to the baby who soon was off to sleep. Suddenly, the little cherub heard the sound of trumpets and he knew he had to return to heaven, so off he flew, forgetting his harp.

"The next day, the baby's mother found the harp and, knowing the value of the instrument, hid it away. Days later, when she was making dough, she decided to cut the dough into long thin strips and cook them. She remembered the harp and she used it to cut the strips. That is how the *ghitarra* came to Italy and how the first macaroni was made."

Il ferro per fare le pizzelle (the *pizzelle* iron) was another one of Nonna's prized possessions. This heavy metal baking tool is used to make Italian waffles or wafers called *pizzelle*. Some of these *pizzelle* irons were in families for many, many years. Some were very elaborate and some even had the family names or crest carved into the iron. Nonna's had only her initials.

The *pizzelle* iron is made of two long, round, smooth metal rods that are welded to two rectangular plates. These plates are hinged together. When the rods are separated, the two rectangular plates open and a teaspoon of the anise and licorice flavored *pizzelle* dough is placed on the plates. The rods are closed and the dough is squeezed and locked in place. The iron is placed over a high open jet on the gas range.

To time the cooking of the dough, Nonna would say one slow "Hail Mary," then turn the iron over so the other side of the *pizzelle* could be baked, saying another slow "Hail Mary."

Nonna told us several legends about how people started using *il ferro per fare le pizzelle*. One story was the *pizzelle* cakes were baked to celebrate *La Festa dei Serpenti* (Festival of the Snakes). Apparently an Italian village was overrun by snakes and when they were rid of them, the villagers celebrated by making *pizzelle*. Another story was that in her home region of Abruzzi, where in fact the idea of *pizzelles* and *il ferro per fare le pizzelle* originated, they celebrate the goodness of a monk who taught religion to the town children in the piazza.

Nonna's own story was that the *pizzelle* iron was created by the Abruzzese to celebrate the defeat of Satan in the Garden of Eden.

"The iron is heated over a high fire to remind us of hell and the iron is heavy because this is the heavy burden we carry from our sins. That is why a Hail Mary is recited so that Satan is reminded of his head being crushed by Mary. The *pizzelle* is made of sugar and anise to remind us of the sweetness of God's love and forgiveness."

Nonna's iron had sentimental value to it. Her second husband, Gennaro D'Amore, my grandfather, gave the iron to her as a gift on their first wedding anniversary.

Every time she used the *pizzelle* iron, burned a big candle in Grandpop's memory or touched the wedding ring she still wore, she would whisper a prayer for him.

Nonna's other favorite thing was her *mestolo*. This was a

wooden spoon that she used for every meal or cake she made. She told me that when she got the spoon it was bone white, but years of use had changed its color to walnut brown. It was almost worn smooth. This spoon was the last thing her mother and father had given her before she left Italy. Nonna often said that when she got this spoon she knew she would never see her parents alive again. Leaving Italy was like a death, but because she had this spoon with her, she felt she would always have her parents with her.

Besides this sentimentality, the spoon had a religious value to it. Before her parents gave her the spoon, they had taken it to Nonna's parish priest in her small village of Rapino. This priest did something that was unheard of in the church: He placed the spoon on the altar the Sunday before she left for America. After the Mass, he blessed it.

Nonna always said that this priest was truly in heaven because he was a man of God and a man whose life was dedicated to the service of the children of God. Because of his blessing on the altar of God, she firmly believed that this spoon was what helped her to be a good cook.

One time, my Mother made a cake for Nonna's birthday. As we were eating it, I looked at Nonna. From the small gleam in her eyes, I knew she did not like it.

Later she asked me if I had liked it and I said, truthfully, "It didn't taste as good as your cakes, Nonna."

She smiled and then asked, "Did your mother use my recipe?"

"Yes."

"Did she beat the cake dough long?"

"Yes."

"Hmm, I can't imagine what went wrong. Ah! Did she use my *mestolo*?"

"No."

"Ah, that's why it didn't taste good—she didn't use my spoon."

In regard to her spoon, she once told us this story:

"Jesus and Joseph were talking one day about what to give Mary for the Jewish holiday of Hanukkah. They were running out of things to give her. They had given her a stool for her feet and a chair to rest on, a small table to put her plants on, and even small shelves on which to keep the wooden bowls they had given her. They had made wooden buckets and wooden trays for her. But for this holiday, they were out of ideas.

"As the days drew closer and closer to Hanukkah, they remained without an idea. Then Jesus remembered that His grandmother, Saint Ann, had a large stick that she used to stir the family stew. He suggested to Joseph that they make a stirrer for Mary.

"Joseph thought for a moment and then said, 'Let's go a step better. Let's invent a new kind of stirrer.'

"Jesus agreed, and the two set out to make Mary her Hanukkah gift. The more they worked on this gift, the more improved it became. Finally they had created a small stirrer with a long handle, a round wide flat end that had a shallow hollowed-out bowl to it. So, the spoon was invented.

"The first day Mary used her new gift, she made soup with it, and then bread, and then cookies.

"When Mary went to heaven, she left this holy and valuable spoon with her friend Martha of Bethany. Martha passed it on to others when she died. That spoon was owned by Saint Helena, Saint Monica, Saint Zita, Saint Rita, Saint Claire and many other mothers and cooks, and it helped all of them to become good cooks. They say that Mary's spoon is still somewhere in the world but no one knows where. That is why all *mestolo* are so important because one of them could be the spoon of Mary, the spoon made by Jesus and Joseph—their Hanukkah gift for Mary."

CHAPTER SIXTEEN

• UGLY HOT PEPPERS •

On a very icy and bitter winter day, a strong, cold wind pressed against the wooden-framed windows of our house and a chilling draft seeped through them into all the rooms of the house. The coal heater was constantly being fed coal and our water radiators were hot. But still the house was cold—very cold. We had learned from experience that on days like this, there was nothing we could do but stay as warm as possible indoors.

On this particular winter day, everyone in our house was sick except Nonna and me. By some kind thought from God, we had been spared the fevers, hacking coughs, running noses, sneezes, aches and watery eyes.

Throughout the house, "God bless you" could be heard a thousand times in stressful harmony with loud sneezes, coughs and low moans of discomfort.

As soon as "the plague" broke out, Nonna ordered my mother, aunts and cousins to bed, and she immediately began her decontamination drill:

1. I was not to go near any of "the sick ones."

2. She and I would sleep together in the back room away from the rest of the house until everyone was well.

3. Each and every dish, drinking glass and eating utensil used by any of "the sick ones" was to be washed over and over again in hot water.

4. All clothing was to be soaked and then washed in hot boiling water.

5. Candles were to be burning on the dining-room table imploring God and any of His saints to help all in our family who were sick. These new candles were added to the perpetual candles burning for our men serving in the military.

"Well, Vinzee, God has blessed us. He is giving us a chance to do good for those we love. Now we are His and their servants."

Of course I didn't find being well to be much of a blessing because I was doing double work around the house. Worse than all the work was the fact that I was the only kid in the house who had to get up early every morning, walk through the cold wind to King of Peace School and face another day under the rigid hands of the Franciscan nuns. Still worse, I had to do homework while my cousins had none.

For two days, I suffered in silence. On the third day, I had had enough of my cousins being so lucky. I decided I would get even with them. That day, I went to each of their classrooms and asked their teachers to give me whatever schoolwork they had missed so they could do it at home. The sisters prepared the work. On the next day, a Friday, I carried all my cousins' schoolbooks and homework assignments home. It was a lot to carry. I felt that my sore arms and shoulders were my punishment for being revengeful, but as it turned out, I got a further punishment: My cousins were not annoyed at all but thankful that I had gotten their schoolwork for them. I wasn't prepared for Nonna's excitement when she heard what I had done.

"Oh, Vincenzo," Nonna said, glorying in pride over her grandson. "I am so proud of you. I would never have thought of doing such a nice thing. Now your cousins will be able to keep up with their classes. Maybe they will get their minds off of being so sick and get well quicker, all because of you."

I dared not tell her that I did it out of revenge. I simply looked at her blankly and wondered how a young boy like myself would ever get to the point of thinking like an adult. How did adults come to some of their conclusions? I walked away from Nonna and sank into guilt.

The next day was Saturday, and Nonna woke early. I heard her moving around our temporary bedroom. I was so warm and comfortable in bed under my many warm covers that I continued to pretend I was sleeping. Beyond the door I could hear "the sick ones" still sneezing and coughing.

"Vinzee, get up and come to Mass with me."

"Oh Nonna, it's too cold to get up."

"And do you think that Jesus said that to His grandmother when she got him up for Temple?"

"Nonna, it never gets cold in Palestine."

"Wise Guy, you think you know so much. Well tell me how come it was cold on the night Jesus was born? Maybe I should have a talk with Saint Francis and tell him he was wrong or better yet, tell Father Cosago that his December Christmas manger is all wrong."

She turned, walked out of the room, down the long hall and down the stairs.

I crawled out of bed, knowing I had lost again.

The morning chill greeted me abruptly, so I dressed quickly and ran from the room and down the steps for my hot cup of coffee, bread and butter. That was God's gift to my body every winter morning.

"After Mass, we will have to walk to a special store far from here," Nonna said. "Get bundled up. Wear your scarf, gloves and extras socks—and don't forget a hat."

As an afterthought, she added, "And go brush your teeth."

As we were ready to leave the house Nonna yelled up to all "the sick ones" in the bedrooms, "We are going to Mass and we will pray for all of you to get better. Then we are going to go and get some special medicine for you. Hot coffee is on the range and there is plenty of bread and butter for all."

She looked at me, smiling.

"Don't you want to say something nice to your mother, aunts and cousins?"

I looked at her with confusion.

How could I wish them well when they were better off than I was?

They were in their warm beds while I had to face the coldest day of creation, I thought.

With all the enthusiasm of wet discarded spaghetti, I shouted up to "the sick ones": "I'll pray for you, too."

We walked the five windy city blocks in total silence. When we arrived at King of Peace we attended Mass in a cold church, but we were used to this because our church was always cold, even in the summer. After Mass, we walked another five blocks to an Italian store where English was never spoken. Here, it was like a piece of Italy had been packaged and transported to Philadelphia.

Nothing American was sold in this store. Nothing American was in this store.

Tony, the proprietor, and Nonna spoke in Italian. She gave him her order, but I did not hear because I was walking around the store looking at all the items on the shelves. I knew I could only look because we couldn't afford many of them. Luckily, I could remember once in my eight years on earth as an Italian having eaten or tasted some of these items. I thanked God for having had those rare times. I walked back to Nonna just as Tony began weighing two large brown bags of red and green hot peppers.

As the storekeeper packed the bag with these peppers, I grew intimidated by them. They were wrinkled, twisted, ugly and mean-looking. They looked vengeful. Just looking at them made me feel the heat of all the angry punishment they could produce.

We left the store and trudged home. The strong wind had somehow found a way under my clothing and it began to wrap itself around my skin. I was certain I was turning blue from the cold. My eyeballs lost their moisture. My feet, hands, ears and nose were soon lost to me; they now belonged to Brother Winter. I began to pray that we would soon reach my cold house and another cup of hot coffee.

Finally we arrived, and after catching our senses we

announced to "the sick ones" that we were home. The response from everyone upstairs was a familiar round of coughs, sneezes, moans and grumbles.

We went into the kitchen, where Nonna reheated the coffee pot. I got the cups, milk, spoon and corn syrup. We were still on war rations and had no white sugar.

One of "the sick ones" had washed the breakfast cups and the bowls they had used in our absence and left them on the washboard by the sink. Nonna immediately put hot water in a large pot to boil. She returned to the kitchen sink, opened the hot water faucet and began washing the cups, bowls and utensils in the hot water. Then she put them in the pot of water to be boiled.

We drank our coffee in silence, slowly reclaiming our numb body parts.

Finally Nonna got up from her chair. "Vinzee, wash our cups."

I gathered our cups and spoons and began washing them in the hottest water my hands could tolerate. As I stood washing and enjoying the warmth on my hands, I watched Nonna as she got her big, wide frying pan, and her two smaller ones. She poured olive oil in them and put them on the gas range over a high flame. With her *mapeen*, she emptied the boiled cups and bowls from "the sick ones" into the sink. She washed the big pot in hot sudsy water and when she finished she began filling it up with warm water. "Now wash everything again," she ordered. I gladly obeyed.

After washing the cups and bowls, I went and sat at the kitchen table and watched Nonna moving around the kitchen, wiping the surfaces of the gas range and the table. I always loved to watch her in the kitchen, because she was always able to find things to do that no one else seemed able to find.

The heat from the gas range with all its jets ablaze made the kitchen the warmest place in the house, possibly in the whole city, so I got up from my chair at the table and moved to a chair closer to the range to rid myself of any traces of chill in my body.

Soon the water was boiling and the olive oil in the pans was beginning to smoke.

"Vinzee, get me the peppers off the table in the other room." I carried the two large brown bags into the back kitchen and I thought I could feel the peppers' nastiness seeping through the brown paper. I put the bags on the table and moved away from these unpleasant peppers.

Nonna ripped open the bags and the mean, wrinkled, twisted, ugly red and green peppers spilled and rolled onto the table. I watched as she cut every pepper in half, leaving stems and seed intact. She gathered a big handful of peppers, carried them to the frying pans and dropped them in the very, very hot olive oil.

The hot olive oil and the cool peppers sent puffs of smoke into the air, and the peppers angrily responded to the oil with loud popping sounds. Nonna put another big handful into the pot of hot water and those peppers let off puffs of steam. With all this popping and steaming, I knew my feelings about those peppers were correct. Surely they came from that far-off place below the earth.

With quick footwork, Nonna continued to add to the three pans and the water pot until they were crammed with the ugly, mean-looking red and green hot peppers.

Within minutes, the peppers surrendered to the hot oil and the smoke from them rose to the ceiling and filled the back kitchen. It continued to travel throughout the house and from room to room like a creeping monster. It started to irritate my nose and sting my eyes. As tears flooded from my eyes, I started to cough. Soon I heard more loud coughing from the bedrooms upstairs.

"Mom, what are you cooking?" I heard my mother shout from one of the rooms upstairs.

Nonna smiled and simply lowered the fire under the pot and pans.

The peppers, resenting their treatment, popped and hissed and smoked some more.

She grabbed my hand and dragged me into the living room as I continued to cough. She reached for the coats, scarves, gloves, and hats that we had just thrown on the living room chairs instead of hanging them in the clothes closet. She shoved my arms into my clothing.

"Come, Vinzee, we have to got get some fresh air," she said, gagging on the foul air of the house.

"But Nonna, it is so *cold* outside," I objected, with stinging eyes and burning nostrils.

"You have no idea how hot it is going to get in here," she said with a slight giggle.

Again, from upstairs, "the sick ones" were hacking and crying out:

"Mom, what are you doing?"

"Mom is something burning?"

"Grandmom, are you trying to kill us?"

I looked at Nonna, and I was surprised to see she was bundled and already headed for the front door—with a total lack of care. Was she just going to ignore the questions from upstairs?

I followed suit, insulating myself in my winter gear and following her out the house.

"Come, let us take a quick but small walk around the block to the park. By the time we get back, everyone should be better. The hot pepper air will open up their lungs. You will see; tomorrow they will be better."

She looked down at me, smiling broadly. She knew something I didn't. I wanted to ask her how those ugly hot peppers were going to help our family, but I was too cold to want a conversation.

The park was a full city block away from our house and at the pace Nonna walked, it would take us only a few minutes to complete our walk.

Defying the cold air she spoke, "You have been very helpful and very good these past four days, Vinzee. I am very pleased and proud of you. I am very happy that you enjoyed helping others, and you really made me proud when you brought your cousins' books home for them to keep up in school. That was very thoughtful of you."

Guilt and shame overwhelmed me. I never liked lying to Nonna and I never liked her praising me for things I had not done.

"Nonna, I have to tell you something."

"Oh, and what would you have to tell me?"

I hesitated for a few moments, sure that the truth was going to bother her.

"I took the schoolbooks home because I was mad that I had to go to school and do homework while the others could stay home and do no homework. I didn't do it because I wanted to be helpful. I did it because I was mad, not because I wanted to do good." I blurted everything out so quickly that I was sure I had made a new world record in speed talking.

I heard a faint, "Oh, I see."

I knew I had disappointed her and wished I could take back what I had said. Though I was supposed to feel good after speaking the truth, I didn't. Being truthful was something that grown-ups did often, Nonna once told me, but now I wasn't so keen about being a grown-up.

I will have to learn how to like lying, I thought to myself and that resolution made me sad. To lie would mean having to tell that sin in confession. My classmates told me that the priest really got mad at kids lying.

Oh, well, I guess you have to hurt people with the truth sometimes, I thought philosophically. *Another hard thing about being a grown-up.*

We walked in heavy silence. Each moment made me regret even more that I had been so truthful. Finally we reached the street corner opposite the park; we crossed and entered the park.

I looked up at Nonna. Her head was turned away and she was looking at the empty trees and the brown-gray grass around us. The wind playfully circled and raced about us and suddenly, I didn't feel its chill. Instead, I was more worried about the long chilly silence between us.

Finally she looked down at me and there was a small tight smile on her lips—it was too cold to smile wide.

"I was just thinking of a story I once heard about trees. I was trying to remember what saint told the story and I just can't seem to remember." She stopped walking and looked at the tall trees in the park. I followed her gaze, wondering what beauty or magic she could see. There was certainly nothing there that could hold my interest. All I saw was twisted sticks, outlines of real trees, whose branches were wiggling like fingers in the winter wind.

"You know, in all of nature, trees are one of God's greatest creations. They do such good things just by being what they are. They probably never realize that just being and just living are so helpful."

She resumed the walk. "Tell me Vinzee, can you think of something a tree does that is so helpful?"

"Trees are where birds make nests," I said, knowing that Nonna loved birds. I wanted to please her.

Her lips slid into a wee smile and I began to feel things were becoming okay again between us.

"So do squirrels live in trees," she added. "Trees also create shade for people walking and working. They cool and refresh people from the sun. Sometimes they become like walls—no, blackboards—for young people to remind the world of love."

I tried to think of other helpful things that trees did but I could think of nothing more. The frigid wind had turned my feet, ears and nose into ice. It had claimed my body again. It was too cold to think.

"There is another thing that trees do that we people sometimes forget about," Nonna said softly and I looked up at her in surprise, for I was sure we had covered the subject.

"What else do trees do, Nonna?"

"They help feed the animals, especially our tall friend, the giraffe."

I smiled. She was right again. *Now why didn't I think of that?*

"Would you like to hear my story now?"

"Sure," I said, relieved that I was back in her good graces and allowed to be her faithful and favorite listener.

"Way back in the beginning when God was making things, He made trees, but He did not make trees big like so many of them are today. He made them small. They had to grow up and become big just like we have to grow and become big. When He made the animals of the world, the trees were still small and trying to grow quickly. God had told them that when they got big, He would tell them what they were supposed to do.

"But they just could not grow bigger. You see, because they were so small and close to earth, all the animals were eating their leaves. The bigger animals, like the elephants, were trampling on them. The little trees just could not replace the leaves on their tiny branches or repair the damage done to them as quickly as they were being eaten or crushed.

"Now among the animals that God created were those who would always be His helpers. The birds were to fly around and keep an eye on the world for God. When the birds were tired and resting at night, the giraffes with their long, long necks were to keep an eye on the world for God. However, there was a problem with our friends, the giraffes: being so tall and with their mouths so high up in the air, eating had been a difficult thing for them to do. The giraffes had to bend down, way, way down, and twist their legs to reach the small trees. And of course when they did that, they could not watch the world for God. God immediately knew He had two problems that needed to be taken care of right away—one, to keep the animals from eating or crushing all the small trees, and the other, He had to make things better for the giraffes. Before He could do anything about it, His most important creation, humans, disobeyed Him. This was a bigger problem so God called on Noah to build his Ark and to gather animals two-by-two. Then God, because He was sad at man's disobedience, cried for forty days and forty nights and His tears flooded the world."

Sensing that it was getting late, she began to walk faster. I picked up my pace to keep up with her.

"With no one feeding off the small trees, and with all that water, the trees began to grow and grow and become taller and taller, bigger and bigger."

I glanced at her, because I knew this part of the story could not be true. She was fibbing. So with great superiority mixed with a bit of glee, I said, "Nonna, if the land was all flooded, how could that happen? The trees had to drown just like all the other things God made."

"No, I don't think so," she said as we began leaving the park. We crossed the street and started back home. She looked at me with a sparkle in her eye. "When Noah sent out a dove what did the dove come back with?"

I had to think back to my Bible history class but then I remembered.

"A branch of a tree."

"Hmm."

I was amazed that she was right again, and maybe even relieved that she was right again. I was equally amazed at myself for having remembered the story of the Big Flood so well.

"So the trees did not drown. They just got very wet. Remember, Noah sent out another dove and that dove didn't come back. It found a tree and a home, so Noah knew that all the land was dry."

She said nothing more. I walked quickly and silently by her side, waiting for more to be said.

"So you have the story and the lesson."

What lesson?

"I do?" I exclaimed quizzically.

"Yes, and we better hurry up or we may find the house on fire along with our sick family."

We were now moving at a small trot.

When we arrived home, the mouth-watering smell of cooked peppers, usually a welcome smell, had flooded the house, but the air had that spiteful sting to it that again irritated my nose and throat. I began to cough immediately. My cough joined those of "the sick ones" and soon my coughs were lost in the chorus.

Nonna rushed to the kitchen and turned off the jets under the smoking hot peppers.

I walked slowly to the kitchen, still reeling from the smell of fried peppers and from the story I had heard but didn't understand. The peppers in the frying pans now looked even meaner and uglier. They had shrunk and withered and looked beaten and mushy, but they still conveyed a defiance that promised revenge.

Nonna, with her back to me, said, "You see, by doing what He did, God solved His problems. The trees grew quickly, so the birds and squirrels were able to make homes. By the way, because of this, God had to permit the lions, tigers, and bears to become flesh eaters. He had taken so many trees out of their reach that they began to starve, so He had to permit them to eat meat. As for the giraffes, well, now they didn't have to bend down and eat. They could continue to hold up their heads, look over the world while eating the tops of the trees, and keep watch for God."

Nonna turned and looked at me, her eyes watery from the stinging air. She coughed slightly to clear her throat.

"The trees were saved by God, and they became the first sign of God's goodness. God's goodness is always more powerful than our ways. His goodness never changes. It never goes away. Even when God wanted to be revengeful, He could not, because He is too good. In your case, He permitted you to do good even when you didn't want to do good. You wanted revenge, so you did something to get even, but it turned out to be a good thing. Do you know why?"

I shook my head.

"Because you are made in the image of God and doing good things is part of your being. It is that part of you that is stronger than doing wrong."

She began fanning her face with her hand and then wiped her eyes with the handkerchief she had removed from her apron pocket.

"I did something mean by cooking these hot, hot peppers," she added, in a choked voice, "but by tomorrow our sick ones will be better. They will breathe better. I knew it was an unkind thing to do, but I also knew it would turn into something good. God makes it good because He dislikes seeing His people suffer. God turned your bad thing into something good for the same reason. He doesn't like bad things. Do you understand, Vinzee?"

"I think so, Nonna."

"Good, now help me begin making supper for our sick ones."

During the night there was less coughing in the house and by morning all "the sick ones" were up and around the house. They were feeling better. Some of them even went to Mass with Nonna and me.

In the way that colds go, by midday I became ill and began hacking, coughing, and sneezing. I was immediately sent to bed. I went cheerfully, knowing that I wouldn't have school the next day or possibly for several days. The thought that I could rest comfortably in my warm bed, while the rest of the family had to go to school and work, compensated for the symptoms I had to endure. In fact, each time I coughed, I smiled with a little glee. The sicker I got, the more comfortable I became.

During the night, I remembered Nonna's story about the trees and the giraffes and wondered what good would come from my being sick.

Early the next day, after everyone left the house for work and school, it was just Nonna and me in the house, I realized that the first good thing was that the house was quiet and still—well, kind of quiet, except for my coughing and sneezing.

The second good thing was that Nonna came up the stairs carrying a tray to my bed with coffee, bread and butter on it.

As I dunked my bread and butter in my hot coffee, she sat on the bed and reported everyone was back in good health.

"I have asked your cousins to bring your homework home," she said with a smile on her face. "It will give them a chance to do something good for you."

Oh God, did this have to be the third good thing? I thought.

I looked at her with a disappointed smile.

"And we will get you better very soon."

"Nonna, please don't fry any more ugly hot peppers."

"No frying," she said with a wide smile, "but we cannot waste good things, so we will have sandwiches for lunch...made with ugly hot peppers."

She left the room smiling.

I had learned another lesson.

CHAPTER SEVENTEEN

• HE MAKES EXCUSES FOR US •

Nonna had a deep secret.

She loved the movies. Even when her secret was discovered, she would not admit how much she loved them. To go to the movies was an extravagance that, for some unexplained reason, she felt should not be indulged. So she seldom would allow herself this luxury. But when she did go, it would take us days and sometimes weeks to get her to stop talking about the movie she saw. She would live and relive scenes with an uncanny ability to remember the dialogue.

When one of us would return home from the theater, we would begin telling her all about the movie we had just seen. She would hurry though her duties and clear the back kitchen table and sit enthralled as we told the story line to her. As she listened, her face would be suffused with eagerness and impatience. So whenever any of us went to the movies, we knew we would have to perform this duty—telling Nonna all about the movie. In fact, she would be anxiously awaiting our return home.

As she heard the story lines of suspense movies, mysteries or dramas, her face would reflect sadness, shock or surprise. When we told her about the funny Abbott and Costello (she loved Lou Costello), Joan Davis or the Marx Brothers, she would laugh so hard that tears would come to her eyes.

The entire concept of motion pictures baffled her mind. She could not understand how the process worked. Because it was beyond her understanding, she regarded it as a wonder. The first movie she ever saw was a silent motion picture with Charlie Chaplin in it. For months, she could not get over what she had seen.

Naturally, her love of movies led her to love the movie stars. She found it amazing that the actors could "remember all those lines and know the end without letting us know about it." Whenever we said we were going to the Breeze Theater or the Victory Theater, she would say, "Tell that handsome Mister Tyrone Powers that I said hello."

When the war broke out and all of Hollywood jumped behind the war effort, Nonna's admiration for actors and actresses blossomed to sheer adoration. Once she said with complete sincerity, "Just think, these great people stopped doing their important jobs of play acting to show concern for our servicemen and how to make them happy. Isn't it great that they can do such a thing and get so many people to follow them? If they did this all the time, they might be able to change the entire world."

Still, even with all this love of movies she seldom went to the movies. Then something very great happened. Nonna felt she had been blessed by God because she could see all the movies she wanted to see, and still keep her secret: movie houses began offering "dishes" with the movies every Monday night. After that, every Monday night was movie night in our family.

On these Monday nights we would go together to the movies. For the price of a ten-cent admission, you would receive a piece of china, each week a different piece of china. One week, it would be a cup and saucer, and the next a soup dish, or a platter or a cake plate. Faithfully, and only for this reason did my family (and many families) go to the movies every Monday. The movies we saw were motion pictures that stand as classics today.

The bad feature to this "bargain" was you could not miss a Monday night movie. Missing one night meant you missed that particular piece of china—you never got another chance and you would never make a complete set. I know of only a very few people who did not make a complete set of dishes. Imagine how many movies we saw in order to get a complete serving for six! Believe me, entire sets of china were collected this way and kept for better days after the war.

So after the Monday supper, dishes were hastily washed and put away. We would all hurry to get ready to go to the movies. There was a scramble for clothing and the bathroom. Somehow, my mother, aunts and the three oldest grandchildren were all quickly ready for the night at the movies.

Nonna was always the first to be ready. She would sit patiently in one of the armchairs with her coat and hat on and her pocketbook on her lap. Under her arm would be a big brown shopping bag in which she would carry that night's "dish" so that it would not break.

When my mother and aunts were ready, we would all walk to the movie theater, get our dish and enjoy the movies. Of course, we were early but that never bothered Nonna. She would sit upright in her seat with her pocketbook on her lap and that night's "catch" in the brown bag on the floor next to her seat. Others would be talking and laughing, but Nonna would sit unperturbed, with queenly anticipation. As soon as the house lights went out, she relaxed and allowed herself to be transported into the screen and another world.

We laughed with Bob and Bing, danced with Ginger and Fred, and cried with Bette and Spencer.

We fell in love with Ingrid in *For Whom the Bell Tolls*.

We made a saint of Jennifer in *The Song of Bernadette*.

Humphrey became the cool hero in *Casablanca*—a movie, by the way, that Nonna thought was an Italian movie because of its title. She pronounced it "Casa Bianca"—and thought it was going to be a story about the White House.

The movies made us feel. We saw the good life of wealth and riches, and we forgot the bad things around us because the movies drew us in.

We went to balls and banquets. We flew across mountains, walked through deserts, and danced on ice. We went underwater and lived with animals. We worked as farmers, doctors and nurses, and we went to Paris, Spain and Brazil. We saw sandy beaches of far-away islands with funny-sounding names.

I remember seeing Nonna's face in the reflected light-and-shadow of the movie screen. When we were seeing a comedy or a cartoon and she heard others laugh, her face would relax into a big, broad smile. If the movie was a musical, her face would become bright and carefree and I could see the dancing reflected in her eyes. If the movie was a drama, then she would look serious and nudge me to ask for translations. "They talk too fast and sometimes say things I don't understand," she would say.

Well, there were times they were saying things I didn't understand either, but it didn't matter—it was the movies.

I once asked her why she didn't need translating for what the actors said in the comedies and musicals and she quickly answered: "What do I need to understand? I hear people laugh; that is joy. I see a person dancing; that is joy. I don't need to know words for these things. Joy never needs to be translated. You just feel it because all joy comes from God, because God is joy."

Sadly, the movies also had a way of making us see the bad things that were happening in our world. The newsreels, with familiar voices such as Lowell Thomas and Gabriel Heater, would show us the war. They reminded us that we still lived in dangerous times.

We saw bombed homes, schools and churches—death all around.

We saw faces and uniforms and emblems that imprinted themselves on our minds and froze them in place. Before our very eyes, we saw the enemy and all that the enemy could do. There was no need for imagination. We had reality in front of us and felt the grip of its cold fingers. It was scary.

Nonna would make it all connect with God. She once said, "When I go to the movies, I often think of God. Like me, He is watching people going through their lives, trying to live life with all its problems and troubles. He is watching and see-ing things we are doing. Here we are, His creation, and we have lost the purpose of His creating us and of His Son's mes-sage. He told us to love but we hate; He told us to have mercy but we are cruel; He told us to be just but we ignore each other. And yet we expect Him to show us love, mercy and jus-tice with no borders or limits. Do you see how sad this is for God? But God has great patience. We often forget that. Perhaps we should learn to thank Him for his patience.

"No matter how bad we are, we are His and He loves us. Love and patience go together like our coffee and milk. Love and patience both make excuses for the one loved. God, because He is both love and patience, does just that—He makes excuses for us."

CHAPTER EIGHTEEN

• I WROTE ABOUT NONNA •

Once, Nonna saw a movie in which one of the main characters died. Her casket was placed in a horse-drawn hearse and taken to the church. For days after seeing this film, she talked about how beautiful that funeral was.

Finally, one day she announced to us all, "When I die, I would like to have that kind of funeral."

A few years later, on May 6, 1946, Nonna died after suffering a long bout with cancer. She was fifty-eight years old. The war in the Pacific was still on. The family wanted to get all the men in our family home for the funeral, so we held her body for five days. They all made it home.

Of course, we could not afford a horse-drawn hearse but we could afford professional pallbearers. They carried her casket through the streets to the church.

It was a warm, still May day. The sun shone brightly, blindingly down on the long procession that extended for a full city block. All thirty-three ladies of the Sacred Heart Society were there, leading the long line of mourners—family, relatives far and near, friends and neighbors.

As I walked down the streets that Nonna and I had walked so often together, my young mind was flooded with many, many memories and some regrets. As I passed by neighbors' houses, I remembered their connections to Nonna.

We passed by Alma and Bernice, the two mute girls who had become our friends. They were standing on their steps crying loudly. I saw them sign, "Good-bye."

We walked passed Freddie's house. He was in his wheelchair in the vestibule of his house. His face was tight and flushed and he was wearing his Army uniform.

We passed by Cathy's house, and she was sitting by the window, tapping softly on the glass.

Buddy was standing on the steps of his house with his hands still, stuffed into his pockets. His head was lowered.

Emma and Joe had opened their front window wide and stood by the window looking out. I thought I heard Emma sob as she waved.

Annie, our May Queen, was standing on the pavement when we passed her house. She had a flower in her hand and she placed it on Nonna's casket.

As we walked out of our street and up 24th Street, my friend Tommy's mother, who had broken her leg two weeks before Nonna died, was standing on the corner with her two daughters, Martha and Lena. She had told them if she could not walk to the corner, she wanted to be carried.

Jimmy, the grocery store man, had shut his store. He stood on the corner of his street watching with silent tears running down his face.

I was so very proud of my Nonna and so happy to see all her friends remembering her. I knew pride like this, God would permit. Even today I am so very proud of my Nonna.

That summer was the hardest summer to live. It was so empty. Every piece of furniture, every room I entered, every utensil I used, every meal I ate, every tick of the clock reminded me of Nonna.

When I returned to school in September, my new teacher, Sister Mary Aloysius, told us our first assignment in English class would be to write a composition on the most important person in our life. Of course, there was no doubt in my mind that I would write my composition about Nonna.

At home that night, I got out a clean sheet of lined loose-leaf paper and picked up Dismas, my second-best fountain pen. In my neatest and best penmanship I wrote:

Her name was Domenica Maria and she was my Nonna, the smartest, the best grandmother and the smartest storyteller in the whole world. She knew everything in life and knew the stories of all the great people and saints that ever lived in the world.

I will always remember her standing by the kitchen gas range cooking for she was the best cook in the world. Under her arm was a *mapeen*, which she always kept near her in case of spills or the need to clean up a spill.

The next day, with great pride, I turned in my composition. The following day I got it back—with a big "zero" on the top of the page.

I rushed up to Sister Mary Aloysius and asked why I got a zero.

"I didn't understand everything you wrote. You were making up words. What is a *mapeen?*"

"It's a *mapeen!*"

"See, you are just making up words. Most likely, the entire composition is untrue."

I was dismissed, and I was crushed.

All the way home I remained silent, and I didn't stop to talk to my friends or to play as I usually did.

When I walked into my house, I broke down and cried.

My mother came into the living room and asked, "Vincent, what is wrong?"

I opened my school bag and pulled out my composition and gave it to her.

She looked at the mark and I saw her eyebrow arch, then she sat and read what I had written. Halfway through the composition she was crying.

"Oh Vincent, this is beautiful. It is so much like Grandmom. You did a beautiful job. But why did you get so bad a mark?"

"Sister Mary Aloysius said I made it all up!" I cried out. "She said I made up words."

"What words?"

"She asked me what a *mapeen* was and I told her."

My mother stood up and carefully folded the composition paper in half.

"Something is wrong here. I am going to go see Sister Mary Aloysius right now. But first you have to stop crying and tell me everything that happened and everything that was said."

So I repeated all that had taken place between Sister and myself.

"And when she asked you what a *mapeen* was, you said what?"

"I told her it was a *mapeen*."

"I see," my mother said. She walked into the kitchen and came back wearing a jacket. She grabbed my hand and we walked back to the convent and to Sister.

I had mixed emotions about this visit. I wanted my mother to make Sister change the mark, but I was worried about what Sister would do to me when she and I were alone. I was certain she would be very angry at me for having my mother bother her at the convent.

We arrived at the convent and my mother rang the door-bell.

Sister Mary Thaddeus answered the door and after a quick exchange of niceties she went and got Sister Mary Aloysius.

As soon as Sister arrived, my mother shoved the composition into her hands.

"I think we have to talk about this mark, Sister."

"I'm sorry Mrs. Iezzi, but I found the mark appropriate because the composition is untrue. Vincent must have made the entire thing up. He made his grandmother sound too smart a woman and too great a storyteller. He made up words that he could not define."

"Well Sister, I disagree with you on several things. One, Vincent doesn't lie, especially about my mother whom he loved and who practically raised him. A storyteller? You bet, she was one of the best, and someday someone will write and tell her stories. As for words being made up, I guess you are talking about the word *mapeen*. Well a *mapeen* is a *mapeen* and I am sure if you asked any of the other Italian children in your class they would tell you what it is. To my mother, me, my family and Vince, a *mapeen* is a good word, maybe not in classic Italian but it is a good word."

"So let me ask you Mrs. Iezzi, what is a *mapeen?*"

My mother gave her a big smile and said, "It is a *mapeen.*"

Sister looked at my mother strangely then set herself on her heel and said, "You still have not proven what the word means or that Vincent did not make up the word or exaggerate the entire story. The mark will stand, and I will expect him to write a new composition, maybe about you, Mrs. Iezzi."

My heart sank to the ground and I wanted to yell at Sister. But I remembered Nonna's high respect for nuns, so I remained silent and suffering.

"Okay, Sister, but before I go I wanted to give you a small gift." My mother reached into her jacket and pulled out a *mapeen.*

"Here," she said as she planted the *mapeen* in Sister's hand.

Sister stood shocked as she looked down at the cloth in her hand.

"Why, it's a dishtowel!"

"No, it's a *mapeen*," my mother retorted.

Sister looked down at the *mapeen* in her hand and slowly a wide smile spread across her lips.

"I see. Yes, now I see, it's a *mapeen.*"

Looking at my mother she laughed and then turning to me she said, "Vincent, leave your composition with me and I will re-read and re-grade it."

Quickly, the two grown-ups began to get friendly. After a few more nice remarks, they said good-bye.

We left and began our walk home. At first, we remained silent, but as we neared the park, my mother said, "Well I think you will get a better grade, in fact, I expect you will get a hundred. After all, you wrote the truth and Sister now knows what a *mapeen* is."

I looked over at the park. Seeing the trees and hearing the birds, I remembered Nonna. I could hear her say in Italian, "Ah, Vinzee, see God is calling the trees to go to sleep and later he will wake them for spring and new life."

"You're right, Mom, but I'll get my hundred only because I wrote about Nonna."